TALES TOLD TO KABBARLI

TALES TOLD TO KABBARLI

Aboriginal Legends collected by
DAISY BATES

retold by Barbara Ker Wilson

illustrated by Harold Thomas

CROWN PUBLISHERS, INC. • NEW YORK

Copyright © 1972 University of Adelaide for the original collection
Angus and Robertson (Publishers) Pty Ltd for this selection and version

All rights reserved. No part of this publication may be
reproduced, stored in a retrieval system, or transmitted,
in any form or by any means, electronic, mechanical, photo-
copying, recording, or otherwise, without the prior written
permission of the publisher. Inquiries should be addressed to
Crown Publishers, Inc., 419 Park Avenue South, New York, N.Y. 10016.

Printed in the United States of America

Library of Congress Catalog Card Number: 72-79797

ISBN: 0–517–50073–6

First Printing

73-13564

CONTENTS

1 About Daisy Bates
8 About the Legends

11 Meeka and Ngangaru
   Moon and Sun
12 The Mulgarguttuk and Mardyet
   The Sorcerer and the Moon's Youngest Daughter
15 Weeloo, Weeloo
   Curlews
16 Meeka, Ballagar and Yonggar
   Moon, Native Cat and Kangaroo
18 Meeka, Wata and Kwetalbur
   Moon, Pigeon and Sparrowhawk
21 The Great Kalligooroo
   The Great Totem Board
23 Jittijitti and the Yungar
   The Wagtail and the Tribesmen
25 Joongabilbil Brings Fire
   Chicken Hawk Brings Fire
28 Irdibilyi, Wommainya and Karder
   Altair, Vega and Delphinus (Lizard)
32 Mooral and Marjali
   Black-and-white Seagull and White Seagull
35 The Janga Yonggar and the Karnding
   The Spirit Kangaroo and the Bush Mice
38 Moolguroorung and Banningbooroo
   Locust and Carpet Snake
40 Woolgardain and Koolarding
   Whipsnake and Mangrove Snake
42 The Yog, Girrgirr and Karrgain
   The Old Woman, the Hawk and the Blue Pigeon
44 Malgar and the Dwert
   Malgar and the Dingo
46 Wanberr and Jallingmur
   The Crane and the Pelican

50 The Janga Dwerda
The Spirit Dingoes

52 Warragunna, Jindabirrbirr and Joogajooga
Eaglehawk, Wagtail and Pigeon

56 The Ngarri Jandu and the Nimmamoo
The Spirit Woman and the Two Boys

59 Wej, Jooteetch and Wardu
Emu, Native Cat and Wombat

62 The Gij of Death
The Spear of Death

65 Bladwa and the Janga Woggal
Bladwa and the Spirit Snake

69 Kolguru and Jindabirrbirr
Little Pigeon and Wagtail

72 Winnini and Kalbain
Emu and Pigeon

74 Ngannamurra Sings
The Mallee Hen Sings

77 Langoor and Jalbu
Possum and Native Cat

78 Lengo and Mandabulabula
The Seacoast Man and his Son

81 Walja and Weeloo
Eaglehawk and Curlew

84 The Jandu Who Hunted Wallee
The Women Who Hunted Meat

86 Joord-Joord the Lazy Jandu
Shag the Lazy Woman

88 Ngannamurra, Milbarli and Yoongga
Mallee Hen, Short-tailed Goanna and Long-tailed Goanna

90 Kweenda, Kwidderuk and Wata
Bandicoot, Sparrowhawk and Pigeon

94 Ngalloogoo and Koobijet
White Cockatoo and Robin

98 Badhu-Wudha and Kurulba
Right-handed One and Left-handed One

ABOUT DAISY BATES

FIFTY years ago, when the great Trans-Australian Railway, linking east with west, was still something to wonder at, the train used to stop for fuel at a dusty little siding perched on the edge of the Nullarbor Plain in the middle of nowhere and called by the white people Ooldea. This was a shortening of Yooldil Gabbi, the Aboriginal name for an underground lake hidden beneath the sandhills of the area and providing a supply of fresh water over thousands of years before the coming of the white man.

Because of this water, Yooldil Gabbi had become a favourite Aboriginal meeting place. Families would walk for hundreds of miles to gather for the initiation ceremonies of their young men—avoiding the Nullarbor Plain wherever possible, for it was believed to be the home of Ganba the all-powerful snake, who lived in its limestone caves and howled through its blowholes when the hot north wind blew.

It was the last of these gatherings, held in 1919, that brought Kabbarli, the white grandmother, to live among the black people at Ooldea. For sixteen years her lonely little tent could be seen flapping above the sandhills near an Aboriginal camp. Every day she would walk a mile and a half for buckets of water, which she carried by means of a yoke over her shoulders. Twice a week she would be standing on the platform to meet the train. Sometimes her Aboriginal friends would be with her. Sometimes she would be alone, ready to join some important passenger for an hour's conversation during the train's halt.

As the years passed, Kabbarli became one of the landmarks of that long journey. Her appearance never changed. Small and slender, standing very upright in the shade of her big black umbrella, she wore, winter and summer, a tailored costume with high neck and ankle-length skirt, buttoned boots, white gloves, and a straw boater with a green gauze veil neatly tied beneath the chin.

White people knew her as Daisy Bates, an Irish lady of education, who had chosen to live with the Aboriginal people in the west as well as the south of Australia. She had grown to love her "black children", as she called them. In her special care were the old, the blind, and the orphaned piccaninnies. For them she baked damper and made sweetened porridge to be washed down with pots and pots of tea. She spent all her money in buying extra rations and clothing for them, and wrote newspaper articles to earn her living while she was at Ooldea.

She had not chosen an easy life. During this time there was a drought which lasted for eight years; rain scarcely fell at all. Game was scarce, and Kabbarli was as hungry and as thirsty as the rest of the camp. Sometimes the heat was so great that she had to retire to bed during the day to avoid it. Once she suffered so badly from sandy blight that she went blind, and was glad of the goanna and snake that her black friends roasted over their fire and brought for her to eat.

She had made it her vocation to record the customs, the many dialects and, above all, the legends of the Aboriginal people. These were passed on from generation to generation by word of mouth. Since they had no written language, these legends were all the history they knew. It was considered an honour to be entrusted with them. Some could be told only to the initiated men of the tribes. But Kabbarli was allowed to hear them all, partly out of gratitude for her generosity to the Aborigines, partly because they thought she was "kallower", a magic woman.

Every night, when the day's hunt was over and the evening meal eaten, Kabbarli would take her notebook and pencil and go down to the Aboriginal camp below her tent to sit beside the fire and listen to the tales told by the old men under the desert stars.

This was the part of her work that she most enjoyed. The narrator would act out each detail of his story. If he talked about an animal, he would go down on all fours. If he described a hunt, he would creep along the ground as hunters do when stalking their prey. Kabbarli wrote about the "quick flick of finger and flash of the eye as the spear is driven home" . . . about the "songs sung during the performance, to the accompaniment of the beating of short heavy clubs on a prepared mound, mankind's first drum".

Many of the legends began with the words "In Dhoogoorr times", just as other stories often begin with the words "Once upon a time".

Aboriginal history is founded on the Dhoogoorr or Dreamtime, when marvellous things happened. Then, it was believed, the world was peopled by beings similar to the creatures we see around us today. From these beings, Aboriginal man developed. Each group or family kept its feeling of kinship with the creature—or perhaps the tree, plant, or even abstract natural object—which had been its ancestor. It became the totem, or, as the Bibbulmun tribe of the south-west phrased it, the "elder brother" of its descendants.

Kabbarli understood the importance of these legends and wrote them down as they were told, word for word. If the storyteller broke off his narrative, she put down pad and pencil and waited until he was ready to finish it. Sometimes this might take days, or even weeks. Sometimes another narrator beside another campfire might finish the same legend. If her notebook were not handy, she would write on the backs of envelopes or scraps of paper. When a legend was complete, she might send it off to an English or Australian newspaper. She would rewrite it, but she was always careful to keep her original copy untouched.

Over the years, Kabbarli's fame grew, and newspaper reporters would come to her camp to interview her. They discovered that she had not been born in Australia. Her bright complexion, blue eyes, and especially her voice, had altered very little since she left Ireland in 1884. Her maiden name had been Daisy May O'Dwyer and her birthplace was Ballycrine, a tiny farmland tucked in beside the town of Roscrea. She used to say that a banshee must have wailed at her birth, because not long afterwards her mother died and she and her brother, Jim, were sent to their grandmother's farm, to be looked after by a nurse called Allie.

With Jim, Daisy explored the hills of Caraig and Knockshegowna, looking for the elves which, Allie told them, could be found beside the brown streams "under a leaf or on top of a flower". Like many other Irish country people, Allie believed in magic and told the two children tales of "ghosties and witchies and doggerel curses". Later, Daisy was to believe that such simple folk had a good deal in common with the Aborigines. When the mists came down over the Irish hills, Daisy and Jim would run back to the safety of their grandmother's farm, glad of the sight of her as she sat beside the spinning-wheel weaving cloths for her household.

Time passed. The tomboy girl became a grown-up young lady who sailed alone to Australia, where she married a young drover called John Bates. Eighteen months later, in 1886, her son, Arnold Hamilton Bates, was born in Bathurst, New South Wales. While John Bates rode behind his herds of cattle, Daisy and her small son visited pioneering homesteads in the different states. Such journeys might hold many hazards. If a river were in flood, Daisy might have to swim her horse across it.

During one such visit, to Tasmania, Daisy heard the tragic story of the black people who had once inhabited that island. The remains of Truganini, the last of the original Tasmanians, were mounted in the museum at Hobart.

Daisy's marriage was not successful. For a while she went to live in London, where she worked as a journalist with the famous editor, W.T. Stead. In 1899 she returned to Australia, on board the *Almora*, bound for Perth. One of her fellow passengers was Dean Martelli, a Catholic priest who had worked alongside Matthew Gibney, Bishop of Perth, assisting his efforts to help the Aboriginal people of Western Australia. Daisy remembered the tragic story of Truganini as Father Martelli told her about the Trappist mission at Beagle Bay, in the far north-west of that state. He told her how Bishop Gibney had been conducted through the pindan, or bushland, by the wild Aborigines known as Myalls, who wore turkey bones through their noses in order to look fierce, but who were really the gentlest of people. She learnt that the future of the mission was in jeopardy, for in order to receive the government subsidy of £5000, they needed to show great improvements.

A year later, Daisy was on her way to Beagle Bay with Bishop Gibney and Dean Martelli to help with the work needed to save the mission. With a team of Aboriginal women she dug wells, planted fruit trees and weeded plantations. To keep them happy as they worked, she taught them to play games such as "Ring-a-ring-a-rosy" and "Here we go round the mulberry bush". The women called her their white sister, and when the mission was saved and Daisy went back to Perth, she left many Aboriginal friends behind her.

While she was at Beagle Bay, she learnt a good deal about Aboriginal customs and lore. She watched the Aborigines hollow out the sand on which they slept at night, heating it by burning coals, so that it would make a warm covering for them. She went with them in search of the nests of stingless bees and to capture a crocodile. She was told about the Windeegur or curlew which called out "Koree bilbil" to warn of the approach of an enemy; and there, too, she heard the legend of Ngargalulla, or the spirit children. Father Nicholas, the acting abbot of the mission, showed her his record of their dialects and legends. When Daisy returned to Perth, in 1904, she offered herself for the job of compiling a history of the Aborigines of Western Australia which the Registrar-General, Malcolm Fraser, had asked for. She began to work on the existing records, but before long she asked permission to live on the Maamba Reserve, in the Darling Range, so that she might obtain her information from the Aborigines themselves. Permission was granted, and Daisy drove out with a police escort and put up her tent on the other side of the creek from the native huts.

From that time until she left Ooldea in 1935, Daisy Bates lived a tent life in one or another of the Aboriginal camps of west and south Australia. Knowing that the different groups were fast dying out, she travelled enormous distances in search of her material. On one marathon, in 1908, she visited seventy towns, and covered a distance of 5,400 miles. In 1910 she was chosen to accompany a scientific expedition organized by the University of Cambridge. In 1912 she was made an Honorary Protector of Aborigines for the Eucla district. Although, to her great disappointment, her historical work was not published, she continued her researches, pitching her tent close to the South Australian border and living alone with more than a hundred Aborigines who had collected for an initiation ceremony.

At Eucla she was instructed in the mysteries of the Aboriginal zodiac and heard the legends of the stars. She put up a telescope and studied the stars for herself, but what she enjoyed most was "to wander over these great distances in company with the Aborigines and hear the wonderful legends of this and that star", watching as they pointed out the Yaggin or moon road "that was made when the moon was human". At Eucla, too, she was made guardian of the sacred Aboriginal totem boards, a unique honour to be given to a woman.

In 1914 Daisy Bates moved east. She crossed the Nullarbor Plain in a camel buggy with three Aboriginal friends, to attend a congress of scientists to be held in Adelaide and Melbourne. Then war broke out. Hopeful that she would be made Protector of Aborigines for South Australia, she made camp at Fowler's Bay, accepting a small pension to look after a group of old and blind Aborigines at Wirilya, twenty-six miles from the present Aboriginal reserve at Yalata. Although the appointment was never made, she was given the responsibility of Justice of the Peace for Western Australia as well as South Australia. This was the period when she first became known to the Aborigines as Kabbarli: as she recorded in her notebooks, the task of the Kabbarli or "Wise Woman" is to settle quarrels and give advice to members of the tribe. Her reputation spread far and wide among the pitiful little groups that wandered along the railway line. More and more families arrived at her camp asking for "Kabbarli tucker".

As a result, the end of the First World War found Daisy Bates penniless. For some months she acted as matron of a returned soldiers' home in the Adelaide hills. But the news of a gathering of Aborigines at Ooldea brought her back to tent life. So she settled down to write newspaper articles and to continue her self-appointed role as recorder of the customs, lore, language and legends of the Aboriginal people. Later, she was to say that the bulk of the seventy legends that made up her collection came from two main sources: the old people on the Maamba Reserve, and the nomadic wanderers who passed through her camp at Ooldea. They represented many different groups and were often the last of their line, a fact that adds greatly to the value of her collection.

Daisy Bates's life work did not go unrecognized. In 1934 she was made a Companion of the British Empire. A year later she accepted an offer from the Adelaide *Advertiser* to write her life story for serialization in the Australian newspapers. This series, written with the help of the noted Australian author, Ernestine Hill, proved so successful that John Murray, the London publisher, published it in book form under the title *The Passing of the Aborigines*.

In 1936 the Commonwealth Government provided Daisy Bates with an office in Adelaide and a secretary, so that her mass of handwritten notes, guarded so carefully over the years, might be transcribed and catalogued for posterity. Her tiny pension made it impossible for her to stay in Adelaide; she moved to a new camp at Pyap on the River Murray and directed proceedings from there.

By 1940 the work was completed. Ninety folios of typewritten pages were housed in Canberra's National Library. A few months later, in 1941, Kabbarli was on her way north once more, this time to Wynbring, another siding along the railway line. Her plan was to establish a centre for the drifting groups of beggars in the area. Some of her old Aboriginal friends came to join her. By this time she was more than eighty years old. In 1944 her health gave way. She was taken to the Port Augusta Hospital and treated for malnutrition.

During the years her collection of legends had been of great concern to Daisy Bates. She was most anxious that it should be published before she died; in 1945 she received a grant from the Commonwealth Literary Fund to put them into book form. She did her best to go ahead with this work, but her eyes, weakened by sandy blight, were unequal to the task. Once again Ernestine Hill came to her rescue. By this time, however, Daisy Bates was a very old woman. The problems of old age proved too great. When she died in 1951, the legends remained unpublished. A duplicate typescript collection had been donated to the University of Adelaide, which I discovered during the course of my research for my biography of Daisy Bates. Barbara Ker Wilson subsequently worked on the collection for several months, selecting and retelling the legends, with younger listeners and readers in mind. Many of the legends were in rough form, exactly as they had been taken down from the written word. The result is this book, illustrated by Harold Thomas, an Aboriginal artist who lives in Adelaide. It is the first published selection of those legends told to the "white grandmother" beside so many campfires in lonely desert places. It is fitting that they should appear first in a book for children. This would have greatly pleased Daisy Bates, who said during her life, "My greatest and best love goes to children."

London 1971   ELIZABETH SALTER

ABOUT THE LEGENDS

Daisy Bates spent over forty years—from 1899 to 1945—gathering the folklore of the Aboriginal people of Australia. The legends retold in this book are a small part of her total collection.

As with all ancient folklore, these are far more than stories told for pure enjoyment: they represent the oral culture of a people, the beliefs, traditions and history of the Aboriginal race. The legends spring from many different parts of Australia. Daisy Bates recorded them at Aboriginal centres in the south-west of Western Australia, in the north, the Centre, and in South Australia; but she was aware that many of the legends had travelled far from the place of origin, as European settlement of the continent advanced, and the Aboriginal tribes became scattered and lost. She has told how in the Aboriginal camps, "sitting by their fires at the hour of storytelling", she would listen to the old men as they related the legends and lore. She writes: ". . . it is impossible to convey the dramatic gesture, the significant 'flick' of fingers or features which accompanied the narration . . . the flash of eye as the spear is driven home, the tracks made in the sand of the hand or footprint of the bird or animal of the story . . . only those who have watched the storyteller can fully appreciate the dramatic recital." Again, she says: "These tales and myths are told by the grandfathers and fathers to their children, and in this way only have been transmitted from father to son throughout the ages of their being; no written record, and in many tribes, no symbol of any kind, helps to keep alive the memory of these traditions. All is oral, and because in many tribes the custodians of these oral traditions have faulty memories themselves, or were careless listeners in their young days, I have had to listen to hundreds of unfinished tales, so disconnected and scattered that it has been impossible to bring coherence to them." She adds: "Some of the myths have been pieced together over long intervals of time and distance, the beginning gathered at one camp, the end at another hundreds of miles away.... Many... have a close resemblance to others heard in regions far distant."

Of the legends I have chosen to retell, some have a moral or practical character, in the sense that they underline, for example, tribal conventions such as the hunting law, or seek to explain natural phenomena such as earthquakes and floods, how man first made use of fire, or why the creatures of coastline and bush have certain characteristics. Some are related to the solar system. Many combine all of these facets. Every legend belongs to the Yamminga, Dhoogoorr or Nyitting times— the Dreamtime of the race: a long-ago period when men first began to inhabit the earth, and when the totem ancestors of the Aboriginal tribes, the spirit snake, eaglehawk, kangaroo, and other creatures, roamed the land. Often, in the legends, people, birds, animals and reptiles seem interchangeable. This emphasizes the Aboriginal's extraordinarily close association with his environment, which in its turn arose from his nomadic dependence upon it.

Some two hundred Aboriginal words are included in the legends. A glossary has not been included, since each word is explained as it is introduced. All are taken from the regional vocabularies compiled by Daisy Bates. Legends from different regions may have alternative forms for the same word.

To explore this rich store of folklore has been a fascinating task. These are marvellous legends which represent the culture of a remarkable and imaginative race.

Adelaide 1971　　　　　　　　　　　　　　　　　BARBARA KER WILSON

Meeka and Ngangaru
Moon and Sun

In the Nyitting or ice-cold times of long ago, Meeka the Moon was the husband of Ngangaru the Sun, and they lived together in a cave called Meeka Darrbi, the place where the Moon goes down, with their daughters and sons and a great pack of hunting dogs.

Meeka spent his days meat-hunting and travelling about the world. Sometimes he stayed away from Meeka Darrbi for a long time. He would take his great pack of dogs with him, and they would help to hunt down the kangaroo and wallaby. When he came home to Meeka Darrbi, he would throw the meat into the cave for Ngangaru his wife and all his children. When he was away from home, Meeka always knew when it was going to rain, and then he would make himself a maia, or shelter of boughs. When the yoongar, the men and women who lived on the earth, looked into the sky and saw a halo round the moon, they would say, "Rain is coming. See Meeka making his maia."

The women on the earth knew that if they looked up at Meeka in the sky, he would give children to them, whether they wanted them or not. Any woman who did not want to give birth to a child was very careful not to gaze upon the moon.

Ngangaru the Sun went out to gather vegetable food each day, mostly roots and berries. Sometimes she would find goanna and other small creatures as well. She would carry the food home to Meeka Darrbi in her kangaroo-skin bag, but if she had gathered a great deal, she would take off her kangaroo-skin cloak and use that to hold the big load.

Here are some of the stories about Meeka the Moon which were told in the days of our demma goomber, our great-grandparents.

The Mulgarguttuk and Mardyet
The Sorcerer and the Moon's Youngest Daughter

The daughters of Meeka the Moon and Ngangaru the Sun lived on moolaitch, ants' eggs, which their mother gathered for them. Each day, Ngangaru would climb out of the cave where they lived with the aid of her wanna, her digging-stick, and go about seeking the food which her daughters loved. When she returned to Meeka Darrbi, her daughters would sift and sift and sift the moolaitch, making a sound of *tik-tik-tik* and *yow-yow-yow*.

Now in those long-ago times there lived among the yoongar, the men and women of the earth, a powerful sorcerer, a Mulgarguttuk. He used to hear the *tik-tik-tik* and the *yow-yow-yow* as Ngangaru's daughters sifted and sifted and sifted the moolaitch, and he was curious to know what the sound was. One day he changed himself into an eaglehawk, and flew into a tall tree, where he could look into the sky and see all the daughters busy sifting. He watched them for a while, and listened to them talking as they sifted, and then he said to himself, "I will have the one they call Mardyet."

Mardyet was the second daughter of Meeka and Ngangaru, and she was very beautiful.

The Mulgarguttuk spread his eaglehawk wings and flew into the midst of the daughters as they sifted the moolaitch, and when he was amongst them he changed into a man again, and caught hold of Mardyet, and took her away to his maia, the shelter he had built of boughs. He put mulgar, loud thunder magic, into Mardyet's ears and head and over her whole body, and he sucked all the blood out of her heart and got water and poured it into her heart to make new, clean blood. Then he made a great smoke and put Mardyet into the middle of the smoke, until it had driven all the bad smell from her, and after this was done he said to Mardyet: "Now you are my korda—my wife—and I will keep you always."

Mardyet was lonely for her mother and father and her sisters and brothers, and at first she did not like the Mulgarguttuk, this powerful

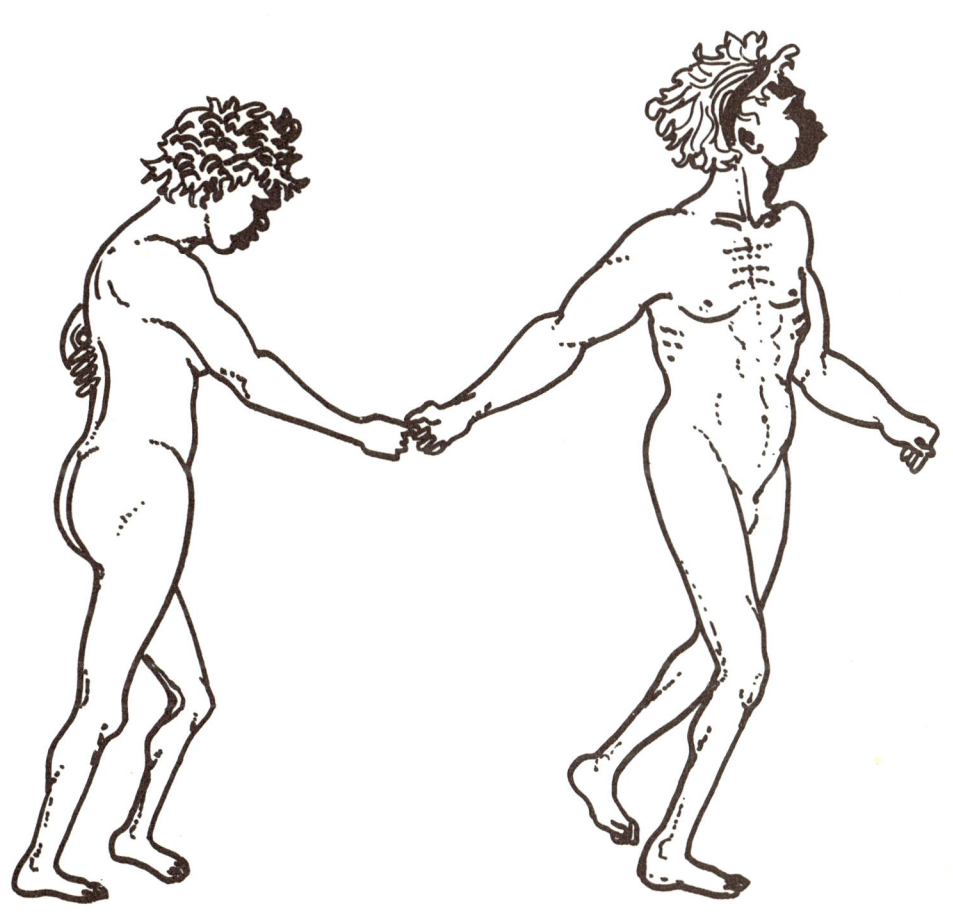

sorcerer who had taken her away to live with him in the land of the yoongar, the men and women of the earth. She wanted to return to Meeka Darrbi. But the Mulgarguttuk watched her all the time, so that she could not run away from him. When she slept he put the mulgar, the thunder magic, all around her so that she could not move. When she woke up, he took the mulgar away so that she could walk about, but he would not let her go back to Meeka Darrbi.

Now Ngangaru the Sun wanted her daughter back again. "Mardyet burrong korda," she said to Meeka. "Husband, bring back my second-eldest daughter." But Meeka was a great coward and did not dare fight Mulgarguttuk the powerful sorcerer.

Then Ngangaru came to visit Mardyet in the maia of Mulgarguttuk her husband, and when she saw how fat and clean Mardyet was, she realized that the Mulgarguttuk was looking after her daughter well, and giving her plenty of food. Then Ngangaru said to the Mulgarguttuk, "You are now the husband of my daughter Mardyet, and she is your wife, and you are in your own country. I am glad you are together."

And in time Mardyet was happy to live with the Mulgarguttuk and no longer tried to run away from him.

Weeloo, Weeloo
Curlews

One day long ago, Ngangaru the Sun went out food gathering as was her custom, wrapped in her cloak of kangaroo fur and carrying her kangaroo-skin bag. She was lucky: with her digging-stick she dug down into the earth around the roots of some acacia shrubs and found plenty of bardi, the fat white grubs which her husband Meeka the Moon loved to eat. Sometimes he ate them raw; sometimes Ngangaru would cook them for him by gently rolling them in warm ashes raked from the fire. Now she filled her bag with the bardi, and brought them home to the Meeka Darrbi, where her children sat waiting for her to return.

"What have you found today?" they asked her as she entered the cave.

"I have found plenty of good fat bardi," she told them.

The children loved bardi as much as Meeka their father did, and they began to ask their mother to let them have some of them. But Ngangaru wanted to keep all the bardi for Meeka, and would not let them have any. All the children except the two youngest ones saw that she had made up her mind not to give them any, and that it was no use to keep on asking for them. But the two youngest children went on crying for the bardi. "Give us some, give us some!" they kept calling in their high, piping voices.

At last Ngangaru became quite exasperated with them. She said angrily, "I'll tie up your heads and cook you for your father to eat as well."

The two little children were so frightened when they heard these words that they fled from their mother and ran right out of the cave. And as they ran, they began to change into two brown birds. Their little arms became feathered and changed into wings, their feet left the ground and they began to fly. "Weeloo weeloo weeloo!" they cried as they flew far away, "weeloo weeloo weeloo!" And that is how the weeloo, the curlew, got its name.

Meeka, Ballagar and Yonggar
Moon, Native Cat and Kangaroo

When Meeka the Moon set out from the Meeka Darrbi, he used to go wherever he pleased, and often he talked and gossiped with the yoongar, the inhabitants of the earth. One day, so long ago that death had not yet come to the yoongar, Meeka met Ballagar the Native Cat as he walked about the world, and they fell into conversation.

"When I die," Meeka told Ballagar, "I always come back again, and when the yoongar die, they will come back again, too."

But Ballagar did not believe Meeka. "No," he said, "you are wrong. When we die and are buried, we shall stay in the ground for ever."

"Just wait," Meeka said. "You will all come again, just as I do when I appear in the sky again like the paring of a fingernail. So you will grow again from your bones in the earth."

But Ballagar still did not believe Meeka. "I know you are wrong," he said in a sulky voice.

Then Meeka became angry and tried to hit Ballagar on the head with his axe. Ballagar dodged the axe blow and ran into a rockhole to escape from him. Meeka ran after him, but Ballagar fled into the hole, where Meeka could not follow him. Meeka was so furious that he gave the rock a mighty blow with his axe, and split it clean in two.

Another time, Meeka met Yonggar the Kangaroo, and they sat down together to talk. Now Meeka was a very quick talker, but Yonggar talked slowly. One day, they sat down together and began to talk about death.

"What happens to you when you die?" Meeka asked Yonggar in his brisk voice.

Now Yonggar wanted to hear first what happened to Meeka when he died before he answered this question, so he said slowly, "Nyinduk wong, nyinduk wong—you tell, you tell", and he pursed his mouth and spat reflectively, and turned his head from side to side, then nibbled some grass while he waited for Meeka to tell him what happened when he died.

But Meeka was very cunning; he did not want to answer the question first either. So now he said very quickly, "Nyinduk wong, nyinduk wong", and he began to tickle Yonggar to put him in a good mood. Yonggar liked being tickled, and he began to smile and laugh, and then at last he said, very slowly, "When I die, I go murra murran—nowhere, anywhere—and my bones turn white as they lie on the ground, and the grass grows over them and covers them up."

Then Meeka laughed loud and long and said rapidly, so that the words all ran into one another, "Birbirung guttuk ngain wernyin warinyin, wernyin warinyin, wernyin warinyin, Barramurning nyin—I die, I die, I sit up again; I die, I die, I sit up again; I die and come alive again and go home to Barramurning, my own country."

And if Yonggar had not spoken first, then all the tribes would have been able to come again after they died, the same as Meeka the Moon.

Meeka, Wata and Kwetalbur
Moon, Pigeon and Sparrowhawk

In Nyitting time, the cold, cold time of long ago, no one had fire but Meeka the Moon. All the inhabitants of the earth had to eat their meat and vegetable food raw, because they had no cooking fires; they shivered and shivered because they had no fire to warm them. Meeka kept the fire for himself and would not give it to anyone else. He kept it hidden in his tail.

Wata the Pigeon and Kwetalbur the Sparrowhawk were uncle and nephew; one day they spoke together and decided that they and their people could not endure the cold and the shivering any longer.

"We must take the fire from Meeka," Wata said. "We must go to the maia where he is sheltering and take it away from him. I know he has it hidden in his tail."

Kwetalbur agreed to go with his uncle, and together they set off for the maia where Meeka was sheltering. But on the way Wata became very sick. He lay down, crying "M-m-m" all day long with the pain of his sickness. Kwetalbur sat down beside him, and presently Wata began to flap his wings. When Kwetalbur saw this, he stood up and cried out, "Beebara beebara", and soon Wata was better from his sickness, and they were able to go on with their journey.

Meeka was sitting outside his maia, and Wata and Kwetalbur crept closer and closer to him, until at last Wata sprang forward and swiftly snatched the fire from Meeka's tail, then ran off with Kwetalbur. Meeka sprang to his feet and tried to catch Wata to get back his fire; but Wata ran too fast for him. And as he ran, Wata put some of the fire into all the trees he passed, little trees and big trees, so that they stood burning like torches. When the yoongar, the people who lived in the countryside round about, saw the trees burning, they came running with glad hearts, shouting, "See! See! Wata and Kwetalbur have brought fire to us! Now we need never feel cold again!"

Wata put a lot of fire into the she-oaks, the jamwood, and the blackboy trees, so that the yoongar would always be able to make more fire from their branches whenever they wanted to. Walja the Eaglehawk, hovering high overhead, saw the fires burning throughout the countryside and said, "I am goort gwab—glad in my heart—to see the fire and the smoke."

But Meeka still pursued Wata and Kwetalbur as they ran bringing fire to the yoongar.

"Give me back my fire!" he called out. "I am cold, cold!" Meeka was very angry; and now he thought of a cunning plan to take back his fire from the yoongar. He made a great flood like a big sea which came and covered the land. He hoped that it would put out all the fires that Wata had started. But Wata had been very clever; he had kept the fires in the trees very high above the ground, so that when the water came over the land it did not put them out. Presently the water went away, and then there was nothing more that Meeka could do.

And now all the inhabitants of the countryside were happy, for they could cook the meat they hunted and the vegetable food they gathered, and they need no longer shiver in the cold seasons. When the women lit their fires each day and saw the blue smoke rising, they would sing about Wata and Kwetalbur. "See the smoke of the fire that Wata and Kwetalbur brought us, see the smoke of the fire!" they chanted.

Meeka the Moon never again had fire in his tail after it was taken from him by Wata the Pigeon and Kwetalbur the Sparrowhawk, and for ever after that he was sulky, and used to hiss and whistle whenever he saw the two of them.

The Great Kalligooroo
The Great Totem Board

In the Dhoogoorr, or Dreamtime of long ago, there was once a kalligooroo, or totem board†, so big that it stretched from the earth to the sky. The womba and jandu, the men and women of those far-off days, used this big kalligooroo as a track between the earth country and the sky country. For in that long-ago time, men and women lived for ever, and if they grew tired of being on the earth, they simply walked along the kalligooroo track to live in Kalbu, the sky country, for a while. They could then return to the earth whenever they wanted. Every day the kalligooroo track was thronged with travellers between earth and sky. In each country there was abundant food; no one ever quarrelled over wallee and mai, meat and vegetable food; there was plenty for everyone. No one was ever hungry.

There was, too, a third country, Jimbin, which lay beneath the earth. All the spirit babies who were yet to be born lived in this country, and they could only be born upon the earth. But after they were born, and as soon as they had given their first smile and become ordinary children, they would travel with their mothers along the kalligooroo track to the sky country and back again.

One day, a group of women decided to visit Kalbu, the sky country, but it was late by the time they gathered their children to them and set off, and they were only half-way along the kalligooroo track when darkness and the cold of the night time came upon them.

"We will make a fire here," they said, "and rest until the new day, when the sun wakes up again."

Now it was very cold, and there were a lot of women and children, and they made such a big fire to warm themselves that it did not die down while they slept, but went on burning and burning and burning, until at last it burned right through the kalligooroo itself, so that there was a great gap in the middle of the track that led from earth to sky and from sky to earth.

† *a decorated sheet of bark, a symbolic painting used in tribal ceremonies.*

When the women and children woke up and saw what had happened, they made a great crying and wailing, for they knew that nothing could ever bridge the gap that had been burnt in the kalligooroo track. Those who had gone Kalbu must now remain in the sky country for ever, and those who were in the earth country could never join their Kalbu comrades again.

The women who had made the fire returned to the earth country with their children, and when they told their husbands what had happened, the menfolk called a council and said, "It was jandu— women— who burned the kalligooroo, and now no jandu must ever again look upon the track their mothers have destroyed. Nor must they make a big fire when the kalligooroo is to be seen in the sky, for then all the Kalbu womba—the men left in the sky—would see the fire and they might be angry and send down a heavy punishment upon our jandu for burning the track."

So it happened that from that time, among the people who lived on the earth, the kalligooroo in the sky was kept secret from the women. They were forbidden to look at the place in the sky where the kalligooroo sat down. "Ngai-u-nongu, ee-lung—I look, I die," they would say, turning away their eyes. For after the burning of the kalligooroo, death came to the womba and jandu of the earth for the first time. If the jandu had not burned the kalligooroo track, there would have been no death amongst their people.

Jittijitti and the Yungar
The Wagtail and the Tribesmen

In the Dhoogoorr times of long ago, there was no sea; there were only waterholes and swamps. Jittijitti the Wagtail lived in a fine, well-watered land, and he found plenty of good things to eat there: fruits, freshwater fish, roots and sweet honey. One day, he went travelling a long way north. He travelled and travelled far from his home. He did not come back for a long time, and while he was away, a group of yungar — tribesmen — came and sat down in Jittijitti's land, even though they knew it was his. They built themselves shelters and lit their fires, and grew fat and strong on the good food, the fruits, freshwater fish, roots and sweet honey that belonged to Jittijitti.

One day these strangers looked north, and saw Jittijitti returning, travelling south.

"The kalleepgur, the one who builds his fire and his shelter in this place by right, is coming back," they said.

Then the strangers went and caught good fish and cooked them, and offered this food to Jittijitti when he arrived in his own place, to appease him. But Jittijitti was so angry with those yungar, because they had come and sat down on his own land without asking him, and had used it as though it were their own kalleep, that he would not touch the fish they had cooked for him. He did not speak to them, but went over to the waterhole where they had caught the fish. Here, he took his biggest spear and thrust it down and down into the middle of the waterhole, then splashed the water all around. And as Jittijitti splashed the water, it rose higher and higher, until at last it covered all the land, and drowned all the yungar who had invaded his kalleep. Then Woggal the Carpet Snake, who was a good friend to Jittijitti, came out of the ground and made hollows in it with his big body. All the water that Jittijitti had splashed about with his spear fell into those hollows and filled them, and that was how all the rivers and creeks were made. The rivers and creeks carried the rushing water to the very edge of the land, where it became the sea. And that was how the sea was made.

Joongabilbil Brings Fire
Chicken Hawk Brings Fire

In Nyitting times, Joongabilbil the Chicken Hawk was a seacoast man, and he was able to make fire by flapping his wings. No one else could make fire in those far-off days; all the people shivered in the cold seasons, and ate their meat raw, for they could not cook it.

Kart-gart, kart-gart, kart-gart: all the womba, the people who lived then, would hear the flapping of Joongabilbil's wings as he rose high, high, high in the sky, then swooped down to set the grass alight. The people would rush out to try to catch the fire while it was still burning, but it always went out before they could reach it.

Again and again Joongabilbil left his fire in the grass; again and again the people ran to catch it; but it always went out before they reached it.

One day, Joongabilbil lit a big marr-ju, a spreading bushfire, and went to the top of a tree to watch it. When the people saw this big fire, they ran out to try to catch it, as they always did, but even that big bushfire went out before they got there. Joongabilbil looked down from the top of the tree. He saw how the people shivered and shivered in the cold weather, and asked them, "Where is your fire? Why do you not make fire for yourselves?"

"We cannot make fire," the people told him. "We do not know how to make it. That is why we shiver, and why we eat our meat raw."

When Joongabilbil heard this, he broke off some branches of the tree where he sat, and gave them to the people. Then he set the tree alight, and the people held their branches in the fire and took them away while they were still burning. And when they reached their own place, they were able to warm themselves and to cook their meat.

Joongabilbil watched them and saw that they no longer shivered, and he smelt the good smell of the meat that they cooked. Then he said, "I will put fire in the trees for always, so that you need never

shiver or eat raw meat again." He put fire in the sandalwood tree, in the paperbark tree, the mangrove, the blackboy, and many others as well, and he showed the people how to get fire by taking branches from these trees and twirling fire-sticks to kindle a blaze. And ever since that time the womba have kept the fire which Joongabilbil the Chicken Hawk gave them.

Irdibilyi, Wommainya and Karder
Altair, Vega and Delphinus (Lizard)

In Yamminga times, a woman whose name was Irdibilyi lived with her husband Wommainya and their two sons at a place called Ngaiyenup, beside the Southern Sea. Irdibilyi's brother was Karder the Lizard, and he sat down beside Wommainya's camp, and Wommainya and Irdibilyi gave him food. Karder was a lazy, slow-moving man; he never went out hunting with Wommainya, but was content to lie by the fire all day. Nevertheless, Wommainya saw that he was always well fed with meat and vegetable food, because he was his brother-in-law, and brothers-in-law must always feed each other and never quarrel between themselves. That is the law of the tribe.

Now Wommainya specially liked to eat bardi, the large, delicate-tasting grubs that Irdibilyi would dig from the tree roots. Irdibilyi always tried to take home some of these when she went food gathering each day, so that Wommainya could enjoy them. Bardi were quite difficult to find, and she would keep them aside for Wommainya and not let her two sons or Karder her brother have any, or eat of them herself.

The two boys used to accompany their mother when she went food gathering, for they were too young to go hunting with their father. They carried little pointed downk, or clubs, that Karder their uncle had whittled for them one day as he sat by the fire. While Irdibilyi gathered roots and fruit and gum, and used her digging-stick around the tree roots to find the bardi that Wommainya enjoyed so much, the boys dug for honey ants and ate everything they found. In spite of this, they always said they were hungry.

One day, Irdibilyi went a long way to find some bardi for Wommainya, for it was the season when they were scarce. At last she found some, which she put in her bark scoop, and then she told the two boys it was time to return home. As they walked back, the two boys began to call out, "Let us have some bardi! Give us some bardi, we are so hungry!"

"No," Irdibilyi told them. "Bardi belong to father."

Still the boys went on calling, and they began to beat their mother as they walked along. Even when they got home they still cried, "Give us some bardi! Give us some bardi!"

"No," Irdibilyi told them again. "Bardi belong to father." Then she said irritably, "Go and find some bardi for yourselves, if you want some so badly!"

She began to prepare the meal over the cooking fire, and felt glad that at last the boys had stopped crying for bardi. When the vegetables were prepared, she called to her sons, but there was no answer. She called again and again and looked all around for them; but there was no sign of them anywhere. Then Irdibilyi called to Karder.

"Brother, go and bring your nephews home," she said. "They have taken me at my word and have gone to look for bardi."

Karder was sleeping by the fire. He had not planned to rouse himself until it was time to eat. Reluctantly he got to his feet and set off to find his nephews. But he was too lazy to go far and look for them properly. After he had walked only a little way, he turned round and came home again. "I cannot see them," he told Irdibilyi as he sat down by the fire once more. "Don't worry, they'll soon come back. I expect they have met their father returning from the hunt."

But Irdibilyi refused to be comforted by his words. She was very frightened. She knew it was an important rule that the boys must never be sent away from the camp by themselves, and she had sent them away when she told them to find their own bardi. She was frightened to think what might have happened to the boys, and she also feared Wommainya's anger when he found out what had happened.

It wasn't long before Wommainya returned, carrying over his shoulder a wallaby he had speared. "Where are the boys?" he asked at once.

Irdibilyi told him how the boys had cried out for bardi and how she would not let them have any, but told them to go and find their own. "But I did not think they would go off like that!" she cried in grief and fear. Then she told Wommainya how she had sent Karder to try to find them.

Wommainya was very angry. He looked at the tracks all about the camp, and he soon realized that Karder had walked only a little way into the bush to seek the two boys. However, because brothers-in-law must never quarrel with each other, Wommainya restrained himself from spearing Karder. He set off to find his sons. He walked a long, long way, tracking and tracking until he came at last to Ngai-yenup water. There, in the middle of the lake, he saw his two boys, with only their heads above water. Wommainya stretched his long beard out towards them.

"Catch hold, catch hold, and I will pull you out!" he told his sons.

The boys grasped their father's beard and he pulled and pulled, but the water was sucking the boys down into the bottom of the lake, and they could not keep hold of the beard.

"Catch hold! Catch hold!" Wommainya called desperately. But in a few moments the boys were sucked right under the water, and were drowned.

In his grief Wommainya took his beard and put it in his mouth, and in his rage he spat it out again. So he returned all the way to the camp where Irdibilyi and Karder waited, biting his beard and spitting it out again in his sorrow and anger.

When Irdibilyi saw him returning alone, she knew her sons were dead, and that she would be killed because she had let them go away from the camp by themselves. Wommainya ran up to Irdibilyi, and when he was close to her he drove his spear through her heart, and she died.

Wommainya could not spear Karder, because he was his brother-in-law, but he said to him, "You were too lazy to search properly for your two nephews and bring them safely home, and so you may sit by your sister." He pointed to where Irdibilyi's dead body lay on the ground. "I do not want anyone to sit beside me who is too lazy to hunt his own meat, or look after his own nephews. Lazy men should sit with women and not with other men."

In a little while, Wommainya died of grief for his two drowned boys. And now they are all up in the sky: Wommainya, Irdibilyi, Karder, and the two boys. On starry nights Wommainya, known otherwise as Vega, stands holding out his long beard to his two sons—the two stars south of Vega in Lyra. Away to the south-east, Irdibilyi, known as Altair, sits with her death spear sticking out at either side of her heart. Karder is there, too, and because he was lazy and would not hunt for meat, and could not be bothered to search properly for his two nephews, he has to sit in the sky near Irdibilyi. He is thin and small and weak, and cries and cries because he must always sit beside his sister. When he looks at Irdibilyi, he sees the anger gleaming in her eye, and always he hears in the distance the loud and grievous raging of Wommainya, who stands for ever beside the lake where his children were drowned.

Mooral and Marjali
Black-and-white Seagull and White Seagull

In Yamminga times, Mooral the black-and-white Seagull and Marjali the white Seagull were womba (men). Mooral came from Joongabbu, the north, and Marjali came from Yalmbain, the south.

It happened one time that they travelled north together, hunting and killing their meat as they journeyed. One day they killed two langoor (possums) with their lanji (boomerangs), which were koorili lanji (being made from the wood of the koorili tree). At midday they came to a group of trees which spread cool shade, and Marjali said to Mooral, "Joong-goo wan-birdim — fire make."

Mooral frowned and said sharply, "Nooroo kanna birdim janna jeera ngang-ga — fire I shall make, but I will speak my own language."

The reason for his sulky reply was this: joong-goo was the word for fire which Marjali's people of the south used, but nooroo was the word Mooral's people of the north used. All men like their own language and think it is better than any other, and Marjali's people and Mooral's people used to mimic each other's speech with scornful laughter.

Then as Mooral made the fire to cook the two possums they had hunted, he said to himself, over and over again, "Nooroo kanna birdim, nooroo kanna birdim", to show Marjali how much he enjoyed the sound of his own speech.

When the possums were cooked and eaten, Mooral and Marjali lay down beside the warm ashes of the fire and slept. By and by they woke up and continued travelling north, hunting and killing their meat as before. At Weera-gin-marri they sat down to make a new camp. And once again Marjali said to Mooral, "Joong-goo wan-birdim — fire make."

This time Mooral became very angry. "I don't want to speak like you! I will make nooroo, not joong-goo. Nooroo is the proper word for fire!" And he stood up, ready to fight Marjali; but Marjali was not

ready to fight Mooral. He lay down and pretended he had not heard Mooral's angry words.

Once again Mooral set to and made the fire, talking to himself in his own language all the time. "I will choose a clear space for the nooroo," he said, "and I will find dry wood for the nooroo; and I will make good hot ashes from my nooroo." And each time he said the word nooroo, he raised his voice. He was hoping Marjali would get up to fight. But Marjali closed his eyes and pretended to be asleep.

So they ate their food and slept, then woke up and travelled on as far as Jeeriba-Ngarrin. Here, as they made camp, Marjali said to Mooral yet again, "Joong-goo wan-birdim." But this time he did not just say it once; he repeated it over and over again, just like a song; for now he was ready to fight Mooral.

"Don't you talk like that!" Mooral exclaimed. "Go back to your own south country! I don't want to listen to joong-goo, joong-goo, all the time!" And Mooral mocked Marjali's speech, screaming out "Joong-goo, joong-goo!" like a woman.

Marjali was very angry when he heard Mooral mock his speech. He said, "You are a no-good man. You are mocking me."

Mooral laughed loudly, glad to have made Marjali angry at last. He said, "I am a man of the north and you are a man of the south. We men of the north are much better than you. We fight better, and we don't talk like a woman." Again he mocked Marjali, singing in a high-pitched voice, "Joong-goo wan-birdim, joong-goo wan-birdim!"

Then Marjali jumped up in a great rage. "You put on reerr-ga—charcoal—and I will put on karrl-mul—white pipeclay—and we will fight now."

So Mooral covered himself with charcoal from the fire, and Marjali got some white pipeclay from a hole in the ground, and they fought each other with their koorili lanji. Mooral was too angry to fight well, and Marjali hit him many times, calling out "Jiraa! Jiraa!" after each hit.

Then, as they fought and hit each other, Mooral and Marjali changed into birds. Marjali's plumage was all white, but Mooral had some charcoal on his feathers. As Marjali flew away, he called out "Jiraa! Jiraa!" as he had called when he hit Mooral. And now Mooral, the black-and-white Seagull, keeps to the north, and Marjali, the white Seagull, keeps to his own southern country.

The Janga Yonggar and the Karnding
The Spirit Kangaroo and the Bush Mice

In Yamminga times, a group of yungar, the people who lived in those far-off days, made a big camp at Dowingerup, in the south-west of the land. It was a good place, with plenty of water and food for all the yungar as well as the animals and birds with whom they shared the land.

Now all these yungar were protected by a great Janga Yonggar, a spirit kangaroo which lived in a cave near by and watched to see that the men, women and children of the tribe kept the laws. And the special meat food of the tribe was kangaroo, because the Janga Yonggar was their elder brother and their totem. The tribesmen knew that they must obey the hunting law and eat only the full-grown kangaroos, for the little kangaroos were as their own children. If they had eaten the young kangaroos, then the Janga Yonggar would have punished them by taking away all their kangaroo-meat food. There was another law that the yungar must obey, too, and it was this: they must never mock the kangaroo, or imitate its hopping and leaping.

Every day the hunters of the tribe brought home the meat food: turkeys, possums, and other creatures as well as kangaroos. Every day the women gathered roots, grubs, fruits and lizards. There were many children in the camp. The girls would go food gathering with the women, who showed them how to find roots and grubs and small creatures with the digging-stick. The boys would go with the hunters on short journeys and learn how to stalk and spear the meat food, how to throw the boomerang and use the hunting knife. When the hunters went on long journeys, however, they left the boys in the camp, to be looked after by the demmangur, the old men and women whose hunting and food-gathering days were over.

One day, the hunters prepared for a journey that would take them a long way from the camp. They told the boys that they must stay with the demmangur. "Do not go away from the camp," they warned their sons. "Be content to play about the cooking fires, for the old people cannot follow you into the bush to bring you back."

The girls thought the boys were lucky to be able to play all day while they had to help with the food gathering, as they always did.

The hunters set out. The boys went with them a little way from the camp, and then they were told to go back quickly to the old people. As the boys followed the way that led back to the camp, one of them said, "Look! Here are tracks of karnding — bush mice. Let us pretend they are kangaroos, and hunt them and cook them for meat."

All the boys thought this was a good idea; they forgot the law of the Janga Yonggar, which forbade them to mock the kangaroo or use it in their games. So they played their hunting game; they found a nest of baby mice, which they speared with hard, stiff rushes; and they carried the dead mice back to the camp on their backs, just as the hunters used to bring home the kangaroos. When they came near the cooking fires, the old people saw how the boys pretended the dead mice were kangaroos. "Do not mock your own meat food," they said. "It is forbidden." But the boys just laughed and went on with their game. They cooked the little mice and divided them among themselves, just as the hunters used to divide the kangaroo meat. Then they ate their portions, and stuck out their stomachs as though they had enjoyed a great feast, and afterwards lay down to sleep.

Meanwhile, the full-grown mice, who had been away from the nest seeking food for their young, came back to find their babies gone. They called and called to their children, but heard no answer, no answer. They looked about and saw the boys' tracks, and followed them, still crying for their young ones. Soon the mice reached the place where the boys had cooked and eaten their babies, and they found nothing left but their bones.

"The boys have killed and eaten our babies, and pretended they were kangaroos!" wailed the mice. "They have mocked the Janga Yonggar. Let us go to his cave and tell him."

Sadly and sorrowfully, weeping and wailing, they went to the cave where the Janga Yonggar lived. The Janga Yonggar came out to see what had happened, and when he heard about the game the boys had played, he was very angry. He strode up and down, up and down, biting his beard and spitting it out again in his rage that the boys had mocked him. Then he said, "I cannot punish the boys, for their fathers are yonggar borungur—my brothers—and they are my own children. But I will go to the Janga Woggal, the spirit snake, to tell him what has happened, and he shall punish them."

So the Janga Yonggar went to the Janga Woggal, and he said, "You must punish the boys, for they should not mock me. If they are not punished, then in time the yungar will stop obeying any of the hunting laws."

The Janga Woggal shared the anger of the Janga Yonggar, and promised to punish the boys. He went with the Janga Yonggar and the sorrowing mice to the camp of the yungar. And here the Janga Woggal lifted up the ground under the camp on his great back, and upset all the shelters where the old people and children and dogs were sitting. The whole of that place was turned upside-down. And then the Janga Woggal made a great lake appear in that place where the camp had been, and all the yungar were drowned. The Janga Woggal drowned the boys because they had broken the law of the tribe, and he drowned the old people because they had not taught the law properly. So Dowingerup Gabbi was made, and it still stands today. It is known as Lake Bannister.

And now, when the yungar sit down by Dowingerup Gabbi, if they look down into the water, they may see, far below, the shadows of the trees and bushes and the shelters of the yungar whose boys mocked the Janga Yonggar.

Moolguroorung and Banningbooroo
Locust and Carpet Snake

In the long-ago Yamminga time, there were three countries: there was the country under the ground, the country of the earth, and the country of the sky. It was during that time that the first yoongar, or men, appeared; and the very first man ever to come upon the earth out of Jimbin, the country under the ground, was Moolguroorung the Locust.

Moolguroorung would live on the earth for a while, and then he would die. Each time he died he would go down to his own booroo, his own ground, get a new skin, and then come up again nice and new.

One day, just as Moolguroorung was coming up again after he had gone down into the ground to get his new skin, along came Banningbooroo the Carpet Snake, who was also womba, a man, in those days. Now until that moment, Banningbooroo had thought he was the only one who was able to go down into the ground, put on another skin, and come up again all nice and new each time he died. And when he saw Moolguroorung appearing with his new skin in just the same way as he did himself, he was jealous and said, "You must not do that, Moolguroorung. When you go into the ground, you should stay there and not come out again."

Moolguroorung took no notice of Banningbooroo's words and made no reply. Then Banningbooroo became so angry that he bit Moolguroorung in the middle and broke his back. And that is why today Moolguroorung the Locust is only a little fellow. Moreover, ever since his encounter with Banningbooroo the Carpet Snake he has had to stay in the ground when he goes there after he dies, for once Banningbooroo had broken his back, he could never put on a new skin again. Snakes are now the only creatures who can go into the ground, get a new skin, and come up again nice and new.

If Banningbooroo had not bitten Moolguroorung, the yoongar would all be able to come up again after they die and go into the ground.

Woolgardain and Koolarding
Whipsnake and Mangrove Snake

In the Yamminga times of long, long ago, Woolgardain the Whipsnake lived in the pindan, the bush, and Koolarding the Mangrove Snake lived in the sea, just as they do now. In those times Woolgardain had no poison teeth, but Koolarding had.

One day, as they were both sitting down together, Koolarding pointed to a tall blackboy tree and said to Woolgardain, "Can you run as far as that?"

Woolgardain was strong and active; he ran swiftly to the blackboy tree and back again.

"Now you run," he said to Koolarding.

But Koolarding said, "No, I am too big and heavy to run. I wish I did not have poison teeth, because when I bite I have to get away quickly before the womba — the tribesmen — kill me, and I am so clumsy that each time they nearly catch me."

"Let us exchange our teeth," Woolgardain said. "I will give you my good strong teeth which can bite but cannot poison, and you give me your poison teeth."

So they did this; and now Woolgardain the Whipsnake can poison when he bites and is able to escape quickly before he is killed. Koolarding the Mangrove Snake can bite, but he cannot poison, and so he is not killed.

The Yog, Girrgirr and Karrgain
The Old Woman, the Hawk and the Blue Pigeon

In the long-ago times of our demma goomber, our great-grandparents, there lived an old woman, a yog, who had fire. None of the other men and women who lived in the land in those far-off days had fire; they were cold, cold in the Nyitting time and they used to eat their meat raw, for they could not cook it. But the yog was able to warm herself when she began to shiver, and there was always a good smell of cooked meat about her maia, the shelter where she lived. The maia stood by itself in a place of sand and spinifex, and whenever anyone came to her to try to get some of her fire, she would scoop out deep holes in the sand, and hide it in them. All the sandhills along Willilambi Coast, in the Great Australian Bight, are heaps of sand scooped out by the old woman each time she hid her fire.

One day, Girrgirr the Hawk and Karrgain the Blue Pigeon came to the old woman's maia to ask her for a little bit of her fire. But as soon as the yog saw them coming, she snatched up the fire and put it under her arms. "I have no fire!" she screamed at them.

But Girrgirr and Karrgain could see wisps of blue smoke coming out of her armpits, and they knew she was not telling the truth. They flew high, high in the sky, so high that they would not throw their shadows on the ground below, and there they hovered to watch what the yog would do next.

They saw her look all around, shading her eyes with an outstretched hand, and then she stooped and began to make a big hole in the sand to hide her fire. Down and down she dug, scooping out the sand as she worked. Girrgirr and Karrgain waited until they could see only the old woman's back in the deep hole she had made. Then, suddenly, they swooped down from the sky and swiftly speared her, and took away her fire.

And after this, all the womba had fire, so that they no longer shivered in the Nyitting time, and need no longer eat their meat raw.

They were glad, glad, and praised Girrgirr the Hawk and Karrgain the Blue Pigeon. And for ever afterwards, when blue smoke came out of the cooking fires, the women of the tribes would sing this song in memory of the time when Girrgirr and Karrgain flew into the sky to watch where the yog put her fire:

See Karrgain and Girrgirr going up, up into the sky, to wait and watch and bring the fire to us, so that we may cook our meat!

Malgar and the Dwert
Malgar and the Dingo

In Yamminga times there was once a man called Malgar, who lived by himself in his own camp, at Yogeragain. He was doggee-doggee—a silly fellow. One day he got up at sunrise and shouted loud, loud so that all the people in that place could hear him: "I am going to travel round and round and round!"

The word he used for round was wungula, and the bush echoed, "Wungula wungula wungula!"

Then Malgar shouted again, "Mad mad mad!" imitating the noise the emu makes. And his voice was so loud and strong that the words "mad mad mad" reverberated across the plain.

A long way off, a big dwert—a dog—pricked up his tawny ears when he heard that sound. He thought it really was the call of an emu. The dwert ran towards the sound and began to chase Malgar, who snatched up his wan (digging-stick), his bwok (possum-fur coat), his koytch (stone axe) and his dap (knife) and ran and ran and ran to escape the great jaws of the dwert. And as he ran, he dropped his digging-stick, and the place where he dropped it is called Wandap Kwedering. Then he dropped his bwok, and that place is called Bwokingab. Still the dwert pursued Malgar, and still he ran, and now he dropped his koytch, and that place is Koytch-koytching waterhole. At the place which is now Dapuling he dropped his dap; at Dulburning he passed water to relieve himself; at Dwailwerding he dropped sweat. By this time he was exhausted, and knew he could never escape the great dwert who followed, followed after him.

So at last Malgar stood still and gave a great cry: "Waiwering!" And the place where he stood is now Werangin.

Then the dwert leapt upon Malgar at Werangin and killed him, and carried him as far as Dwertakin, where he devoured him. And at Dwertakin there are two big stones known as dwert bukal—the dog's back.

Wanberr and Jallingmur
The Crane and the Pelican

In Yamminga times, Wanberr the Crane was a man of the bush and Jallingmur the Pelican was a man of the seashore. One day they met and went fishing together around the mangrove swamp. Wanberr was in luck; he got a big kingfish. But he did not tell Jallingmur about his fine catch; he broke the fish in two and hid it in his hunting bag.

At the end of the day, as they were setting off to make their camps, Jallingmur saw how Wanberr's hunting bag bulged. "What have you got in your bag?" he asked.

"It is nothing. It is only a little fish," Wanberr told him.

But Jallingmur knew that it must be a very big fish. "Wanberr is a greedy fellow," he said to himself. "He wants to keep that big fish for himself."

Then each of them made his own fire, Wanberr on the bush side of the mangrove swamp, Jallingmur on the sea side, and they sat down and camped by their fires for a while.

Wanberr made a big fire and put the two halves of his kingfish on it to cook. He thought that Jallingmur would not know what he was doing, because when men made their own fires and camped by themselves, they always turned their backs on each other. But Jallingmur knew what Wanberr was doing. He knew he was cooking that big fish he had caught. While the fish was still baking in the hot ashes, Jallingmur called over to Wanberr, "Let us make a nooloo — a dance!"

"Ngow-ai — all right," Wanberr replied.

Then Jallingmur called to the little Jeeoo, which is now a bird that lives in the mangrove swamps, but was a man in those times. "Jeeoo, sing for our nooloo!" he said.

Jeeoo was always happy to please Jallingmur, so he began to sing, and then Jallingmur and Wanberr danced. As they were dancing, Jeeoo heard the fish crackling in Wanberr's fire. Jeeoo stopped singing to call to Wanberr, "Koo!" He wanted to warn him that the food he was cooking was burning.

But Wanberr took no notice, and went on dancing. At last, when the dance was ended, Jallingmur said to Wanberr, "That was not a little fish you had in your hunting bag. It was a big fish. Jeeoo heard it crackling on your fire, and that is why he called out 'Koo!' Let us fight now, using our fire-sticks!"

As Jallingmur spoke, he picked up a fire-stick from his fire and threw it at Wanberr the Crane, and it burned his legs and scattered ash on his body. And that is how the crane got his red legs and his ash-coloured feathers.

Then Wanberr ran to his fire and picked up a big fire-stick, and threw it at Jallingmur the Pelican, and it broke both his legs. And that is why the pelican cannot go quickly, but must always waddle along the ground.

Wanberr was angry with Jeeoo, because he had called out "Koo!" when he heard the big fish crackle on the fire, and so he hit Jeeoo with his fire-stick and broke his arm. And that is why Jeeoo is such a little bird, and can never go into deep water, but has always to stay in the shallows.

Long afterwards, when the Yamminga times were far away in the past, men danced this corroboree of the time when the crane and the pelican were men, and they always sang this song:

Leave alone the spear!
Fight with fire-sticks!

The Janga Dwerda
The Spirit Dingoes

In Yamminga times there was a spring of clear water at a place called Nyeerrgoo. It was known as Nyeerrgoo Gabbi—Nyeerrgoo Water. The spring was inside a cave which had a long, sloping roof. Two Janga Dwerda, spirit dogs, were the guardians of the spring, and they watched to see that everyone who came to the cave obeyed the law that had been laid upon the tribes when Nyeerrgoo Gabbi was first made. The law was this: anyone who came to fetch water from the spring must take off his cloak and every ornament on his body and enter the cave naked. When he reached the place where the spring was, he must pick up a stone and strike the surface of the water. Immediately, the water would rise up and up, and then the water-bringer could fill his vessel to the brim as he ran back to the cave entrance. If the rising water overtook him as he ran, he would die.

All the Nyeerrgoo yungar, the people who belonged to Nyeerrgoo, observed this law; they always took off their kangaroo-skin cloaks and their ornaments of bone or string or shell before they went inside the cave.

One day some relations of the Nyeerrgoo yungar came to visit them. They went hunting together, and caught many kangaroos as well as other meat food. As the hunting party returned to camp, it passed by Nyeerrgoo Gabbi. One of the strangers was so hot and thirsty that he decided to go into the cave to drink from the spring. Although the Nyeerrgoo yungar had told the strangers of the two spirit dogs that guarded Nyeerrgoo Gabbi, and of the law that must be obeyed, this young hunter ran straight into the cave still wearing his possum-string belt. He drank of the water, then returned with the rest of the hunting party to the camp, where he sat down by the fire and waited for his food. When he had eaten, he lay down to sleep. But he could not sleep, because he began to hear two dogs howling and howling in his ears.

He sat upright and said to the man who lay on the other side of the fire, "Why are those dogs howling and howling?"

"I cannot hear any dogs," the other man said sleepily.

"I can! I can!" the young hunter replied. "They are very close."

"There are no dogs howling," the other man repeated. "Do you think I am deaf?"

Then the young hunter knew that the Janga Dwerda, the spirit dogs of Nyeerrgoo Gabbi, were angry with him for disobeying the law of the cave, and that it was their voices that he heard howling and howling.

"Stop howling! Stop howling!" he cried, covering his ears with both his hands. But the dogs howled unceasingly, and he could not shut out the noise they made. He moved to another part of the camp and lay down beside another fire to try to sleep; still the howling of the Janga Dwerda sounded close in his ears. Then the young hunter jumped up and ran away; but the howling followed him wherever he went. He became hot and feverish; his hands were dry and his limbs felt weak. All that night, all the next day and the next, the howling fell upon his ears, until he could bear it no longer. When the third sun came up, the young hunter was dead.

And that is how the Janga Dwerda punished all those who broke the law of Nyeerrgoo Gabbi.

Warragunna, Jindabirrbirr and Joogajooga
Eaglehawk, Wagtail and Northern Pigeon

In Yamminga times, Warragunna the Eaglehawk was kogga (uncle) to Jindabirrbirr the Wagtail, and Joogajooga the Northern Pigeon. Every day the uncle and his two nephews would go together to seek the sweet geerbaiju (honey of the native bees). The bees were so small that only Jindabirrbirr and Joogajooga, with their sharp young eyes, could follow their flight as they went to the hollows in the trees where they had their nests. Sometimes Jindabirrbirr would catch one of the bees and attach a tiny piece of downy white feather to its back with a drop of blood drawn from his arm. Then he would let the bee go, and it was easy for the boys to follow the white mark as it flew to the hollow high up in the trees where it had its nest.

When they discovered where the nests lay, they would show their uncle, and Warragunna would climb up to get the honey stored in each one: neither Jindabirrbirr nor Joogajooga could climb so high or so easily as Warragunna, their kogga.

Warragunna would climb from branch to branch until he reached the nest high in the tree, and there he would find plenty of sweet geerbaiju stored away. But Warragunna was a greedy man, and when he found the honey, he used to cram most of it into his mouth and eat it, and send down to the boys only leda (bees' fat) and ooba (bees' eggs).

Jindabirrbirr and Joogajooga, waiting at the foot of the tree, were always surprised and disappointed when nothing but leda and ooba came out of the big trees. They would seek out more nests in larger trees: nests so large that when they stood still to listen, they could hear the many, many bees in the hollow, busy storing away the honey they had collected.

"Here, surely, is a tree with much geerbaiju," they would tell Warragunna; and once again they would show him where the nests were in the hollows high above their heads. But, just as so many times before, Warragunna would eat most of the honey himself, and give his nephews only the leda and the ooba, and perhaps a very, very small amount of geerbaiju.

The result of all this was that Warragunna grew fat and strong, because he ate so much sweet honey, while Jindabirrbirr and Joogajooga became thin and weak, and always felt hungry. At last the two boys grew tired of helping their uncle to find big trees which held, as they thought, so little honey in their hollows.

"Let us hunt langoor (possums) and koordi (lizards) instead," Jindabirrbirr said to Joogajooga. "Our uncle will kill them for us when we have tracked them down, for we are not strong enough to kill them ourselves."

So now the uncle and his two nephews went hunting langoor and koordi each day. The boys were skilful at tracking, and when they found a langoor or koordi hole, they would call to Warragunna and ask him to kill the creatures for them. Warragunna would do this, but he ate all the fat langoor and koordi himself, and gave the two boys only the thin ones, which had scarcely a mouthful of flesh on them.

Now Warragunna grew fatter and sleeker than ever, and at last the two boys began to suspect that he was cheating them.

"Warragunna must have been eating all the honey in the trees himself," Jindabirrbirr said to Joogajooga, "and now he is eating all the fat langoor and koordi he finds, and he is only giving us the thin ones. Yet he would not be able to find either the honey or the langoor and koordi without our help, and we should all share the food fairly. How shall we punish him for not giving us our proper share of the food?"

Joogajooga thought a moment. "Come," he said, "I will show you how we may punish our kogga Warragunna for cheating us."

Joogajooga led Jindabirrbirr to some good koordi ground, and here he made a deep hole which looked just like a koordi nest.

"Now you get a hard stick and give it a sharp point," he told Jindabirrbirr.

When this was done, Joogajooga stuck the stick firmly in the bottom of the hole he had made, with the sharp point upwards. Then they returned to their camp.

Next day Warragunna and the two boys went out hunting as usual, and they led their uncle to the koordi hole they had made. Warragunna went over to it and stamped his foot down into the hole very hard and swiftly, as he always did, to kill the koordi which he thought would be inside it. But instead of a koordi, there was the sharp pointed stick, which ran up through Warragunna's foot. He cried out in a loud voice with the pain, and his foot swelled and swelled, and he became very sick.

Jindabirrbirr and Joogajooga were glad to hear their uncle cry. "He has been cheating us all the time," they told each other. "When we found good honey, he took it all for himself and gave us only leda and ooba, and when we found fat langoor and koordi, he took all the fat meat and gave us only thin, no-good meat." And so they sat at a little distance and listened to Warragunna's cries.

By and by they heard Warragunna call out, "Koordurwain, Koordurwain!"

Now Koordurwain, the native companion, was a sorcerer, and Warragunna was calling to him to come and take the sharp pointed stick out of his foot. Koordurwain was in a far-away camp, but because he was a sorcerer, he heard Warragunna calling to him. He came hurrying to the place where Warragunna lay, and pulled the stick out of his foot. As soon as he did so, water came gushing out of the hole in Warragunna's foot. It flowed and flowed from the foot until it made a great rushing river. Then Warragunna died, but his foot went up into the sky, and today it can still be seen shining there. It is the constellation that has become known as the Southern Cross; but to the Aborigines who first heard the story of Warragunna, Jindabirrbirr and Joogajooga, it was known as Warragunna's nimbal, or foot.

The Ngarri Jandu and the Nimmamoo

The Spirit Woman and the Two Boys

In Yamminga times, the people who lived in the north-west of the land used to fear Ngarri, the spirits that haunted the bush. Ngarri were white and dazzling, like the sun; sometimes they took the form of a huge woman, and went through the bush shouting shrilly, as a woman shouts. Sometimes they took the form of an enormous man, and then they made a noise like the kallee-gooroo, the big bull-roarer that was swung round and round at the initiation ceremonies.

It happened one day in that far-off time that two nimmamoo — two boys who had had their noses pierced with sharp pieces of bone — went out to gather honey, the sweet geerbaiju made by the bees. One of the boys carried a little bowl hollowed from blackwood to hold the honey. They saw the bees gathering nectar, and tried to follow their flight when they left the flowers, so that they might find their store of honey. But the bees were so small that the boys could not see where they went. Then one of the nimmamoo caught a bee and held it carefully between his finger and thumb, his hand's mother. He pricked his arm with a thorn, and with a drop of blood he fastened a tiny fragment of white down from the base of a bird's feather to the bee's back. And now the boys could follow that single bee on its flight, and it showed them where the honey was stored. It flew to a hollow tree, and when the boys listened carefully, standing with one ear pressed against the trunk, they could hear the bees humming, humming busily inside the tree. Then they climbed the tree and took as much honey as they needed.

In this way they discovered many stores of honey in different trees, and towards the end of the day their wooden bowl was almost full. They decided to climb one more tree before returning to the camp, and they both went up into its branches. Neither of the boys was aware that all this time a Ngarri Jandu, a spirit woman, had been tracking and tracking them as they went from tree to tree. But when they climbed down from this last tree, they found her standing at its foot, waiting for them. They were terrified, and began to cry aloud. Tears fell down their cheeks like rain. But the Ngarri Jandu showed no pity. She carried a big, big bark vessel under her arm, and she caught hold of both the nimmamoo and put them inside it. Then she took them to the tall, tall tree that was her home. It was a hollow tree, and she thrust them inside it, and covered the opening with a piece of bark. The boys found themselves alongside many ngarri babba, spirit boys, who had once been nimmamoo like themselves, and who had all been captured by the Ngarri Jandu.

Then the Ngarri Jandu went out hunting. She found possums, snakes, and goannas, and brought this meat food back to the tree, to feed the nimmamoo and the ngarri babba. She wanted to make them fat, fat enough for her to eat. Every day she went out hunting; every day she ate the fattest of the ngarri babba. The two nimmamoo knew that soon they, too, would become ngarri babba, and then it would be their turn to be eaten. They were desperate to escape, and sat thinking and thinking how they might do this.

One morning, when the Ngarri Jandu had left the tree to go hunting, the nimmamoo pulled the nose-bones from their noses. The bones were hollow, and they blew through them onto the bark that covered the opening of the tree. The older nimmamoo tried first. He blew and blew until his cheeks swelled, but he could not move the bark. Then the younger nimmamoo blew through his nose-bone, and suddenly the bark fell away. Both the boys leapt out of the tree and fled koonian (north) towards their own camp.

The Ngarri Jandu was far, far away, hunting meat and looking for more boys to bring to her tree. When she returned at the end of the day, she saw the bark fallen away and soon discovered that the nimmamoo had escaped. She was very angry. She tracked them and tracked them, always moving koonian, koonian.

As the two boys ran towards their camp, they met a band of hunters.

"A Ngarri Jandu is following us. Spear her so that she may not catch us!" they called imploringly.

"Ngow-ai—it shall be done," the hunters answered.

When the Ngarri Jandu came along the way the boys had gone, the hunters rushed at her. They threw spear after spear, and hit her again and again with their clubs, but they could not kill her, because she

57

was ngarri. One spear flew in her right eye, but it was like a stone. Her whole body was hard as rock; spears and clubs could not harm her, though the hunters fought her until sundown. Weary and weak, they laid down their weapons at last and let her pass.

So the Ngarri Jandu went on through many places, still tracking the two nimmamoo. And in each camp she came to, the womba (men) fought against her with their spears and clubs. But still they could not harm her. But when the Ngarri Jandu came to the last camp of all, one of the womba there flung a spear which had mirrooroo (magic) in it, and this spear hit the instep of her foot, where her heart was, and so she died.

Yool-burroo boora . . . all these things happened a long time ago.

Wej, Jooteetch and Wardu
Emu, Native Cat and Wombat

In the Yamminga times of long ago, Jooteetch the Native Cat and Wej the Emu were husband and wife, and lived together. Every day Jooteetch went hunting. He used to bring home plenty of kangaroo, for he was a great hunter. Wej went out each day, as well, searching for roots, seeds and fruit. Often she would gather a lot of yams and pound them between two stones to make good cakes for Jooteetch.

One day, while Jooteetch was out hunting, Wardu the Wombat walked out of the trees and came into Jooteetch's camp while Wej was there by herself. Wardu spoke to Wej and asked her if she would lie with him as though he were her husband. Wej said she would do this, and so she lay with Wardu. As the sun's shadow lengthened, she told Wardu, "You must go now, for if my husband finds you here he will surely kill us both."

Wardu rose up, but before he left the camp, he covered Wej all over with murdur — the precious red clay used for decoration in the corroborees.

As dusk fell, Jooteetch returned from his hunting. It had been a good hunting day; the birds he had killed hung from his belt, swinging against his legs as he walked, and he carried a wallaby over his shoulder. As soon as he saw Wej covered in the red clay, he asked, "Where did you get that murdur?"

"Oh," Wej told him, "I found it."

"I don't believe you," Jooteetch said. He knew she was concealing something from him; and he had seen Wardu's tracks in the soft earth. He asked and asked Wej how she had got the red clay, and at last she broke down and told him the truth: how Wardu had come to the camp, and how they had lain together.

Then Jooteetch said, "Make a fire."

And when Wej had made a big fire and it was burning fiercely, he caught hold of her and flung her into the midst of it. But Wej flew out of the fire and went up, up to the sky, where she became Wej Mor—the dark patch in the Milky Way. However, her arms were burnt a little bit before she escaped from the fire, and now the emu has little wings and cannot fly.

Jooteetch was afraid when Wej flew up to the sky. He cried out, "Jooteetch! Jooteetch!" and ran into a hole. And now all native cats make their homes in holes in the ground.

Afterwards, Jooteetch tracked Wardu to his own camp, but Wardu had gathered together a big crowd of brothers, and they chased Jooteetch with their spears, and hit him many times. And that is why the native cat is covered with white spots. Jooteetch hit Wardu on the back, and that is why all wombats have flat backs.

The Gij of Death
The Spear of Death

In the far-off Yamminga times, so long ago that death was not yet known to the yoongar, the men and women of the earth, an old man and woman lived at Ngangalup with their only son. Each day the old man went out hunting for food. One morning he stalked an emu across the plain, and when he came near it he cast his spear. But the spear missed the emu and flew far, far away, and so the old man lost his quarry, and thought he had lost the spear, too.

But as he looked into the distance, shading his eyes with one hand, to see where his spear had gone, he suddenly beheld it returning at full speed, and coming straight towards him. He dodged the spear as it reached him, only to find that it turned and came towards him again: and when he dodged it a second time, once more it threatened him, so that he had to keep dodging it again and again and again; and each time he hoped that it would go away and leave him alone. He knew that if he misjudged the direction of the spear by only a fraction, it would go straight through his body and kill him.

After a while the old man grew very tired with this continual dodging of the spear; then his son came running to him, and when the young man saw what was happening, he said, "Let me take your place, father, for you are growing very tired."

Although he was exhausted, the old man replied, "No, my son. You might be speared, for you are not so experienced in the arts of hunting as I am."

"Let me take your place for only a little while, so that you can rest," the boy pleaded.

At last the old man agreed to let his son take his place, and while he rested beneath a tree, the young man began to dodge the tireless spear as it came hissing towards him again and again. Alas, the son was not as experienced as the father in judging direction and distance;

he let the spear come too close to him, and it pierced his body and he died.

The old man and woman, full of grief, buried their son in the ground, and soon afterwards they went to live in another place.

If the boy had not been speared, then for ever afterwards all the yoongar would have been able to dodge any spear that was thrown at them, and moreover they would never have known death at all.

After the death of the boy the law of the tribe decreed that the place where he was killed by the spear must always be strewn with fresh blackboy rushes by any of the yoongar who passed that way; any old rushes that lay there must first be removed before the fresh ones were put down. And if anyone neglected this law, then in a short while he would die.

Bladwa and the Janga Woggal
Bladwa and the Spirit Snake

Kura, kura, long, long ago there was a man called Bladwa who lived at Nyeerrgoo Gabbi. He had two wives, and the three of them lived very well together. Each day Bladwa would go out to hunt possum, kangaroo and other game, while his two wives gathered roots, berries, fruits, ants and lizards with their digging-sticks.

Now Bladwa's borungur, his "elder brother" or totem, was Woggal the Carpet Snake. It was Woggal who protected him. And this meant that the meat Bladwa enjoyed to eat most was woggal—for that is the law of the tribe. Each man eats of his own meat. But Bladwa was careful to eat only full-grown woggal, for he knew that the young woggal must never be killed: they were his koolongur (children), and he must protect them. If Bladwa had eaten young woggal, then the Janga Woggal, the great spirit snake who lived in a waterhole and looked after all his tribe, would have taken away all the woggal from the hunting ground as a punishment.

One day Bladwa set out for his day's hunting as usual, and soon he tracked down two kangaroos, and speared them both. He was glad, glad to have had such good hunting while the day was still young, and he began to return to his camp. Suddenly a man of another tribe, whom Bladwa knew as an enemy, ran out of the bush and hurled his spear at him. The spear pierced Bladwa's ribs; he threw down the kangaroos he was carrying and tried to pull out the spear, but he only succeeded in breaking it off where it was sticking out of his body. He ran, ran to his camp, where his women were kindling the cooking fire. They tried and tried to pull the spear-head out of Bladwa's body, but it had broken off so short that they could not get a grip on it. Tears were falling down their cheeks in their sorrow for Bladwa's wound.

At last Bladwa said. "It is no use. You are pulling and pulling, but you cannot get the spear out of my body. I must go to the waterhole where my borungur, the Janga Woggal, sits down, and I will ask him to make me well."

His wives accompanied him as he went to the waterhole, the home of the Janga Woggal. It was deep, deep. A big log had fallen down beside the waterhole, and lay half-way across it.

Bladwa stood at the water's edge. "N'ga! N'ga!" he called.

Slowly the waters stirred, stirred until a great whirlpool had formed, and at last the huge head of the Janga Woggal emerged, and the great snake rose up out of the water to see who had shouted. It was different from all other woggal, for its broad back was covered with sleek feathers.

Bladwa walked alone along the long log that lay across the pool. As he walked, the waters rose high, high over the log. By the time he reached the middle of the pool, it had reached his chest. His two women stood on the bank and watched him fearfully. Then Bladwa turned to them, held up three fingers, and pointed to the place where the sun sits down in the second half of the day. In this way they knew that he would return to them in the second half of the third day. Then he stepped onto Janga Woggal's broad, feathery back, and immediately the waters stirred again, and the Janga Woggal went down into the centre of the whirlpool with Bladwa on its back. The water covered Bladwa's eyes and closed over his head, and when he had finally disappeared, the surface of the pool became quiet and smooth once more.

The Janga Woggal took Bladwa to its home at the bottom of the waterhole, and laid him on a heap of soft feathers which it had cast off. Then the Woggal pulled the spear from Bladwa's body and cleaned the wound with its tongue, and curled itself round and round Bladwa to keep him warm and safe. For there were other woggal at the bottom of the pool which came swimming towards Bladwa and tried to bite him; but the Janga Woggal did not let them touch him, and licked and licked his wound until it was healed.

At the end of three days Bladwa said, "Now I must return to my women and my own place."

As Bladwa's two yogga (wives) waited and watched on the bank beside the waterhole, on that third day they saw the surface of the water stir and stir once more as the Janga Woggal brought Bladwa back to them. They were gwabba gwabba—glad, glad—as Bladwa

stepped off the Woggal's back onto the log and walked towards them. And they saw that his spear wound was quite healed. So they returned to their camp.

After that time, the waterhole of the Janga Woggal became a forbidden place, where no stranger might go to drink. If he did so, he would surely die. And all the people who belonged to that place had to strew rushes on the bank of the waterhole, on the spot where Bladwa stepped off the log to re-join his wives. If they did not obey this law, they would offend the Janga Woggal and then they would surely fall ill and die.

Yool-burroo boora . . . all these things happened a long time ago.

Kolguru and Jindabirrbirr
Little Pigeon and Wagtail

In Yamminga times, there were two women of the north, Kolguru the little Pigeon and Jindabirrbirr the Wagtail. They made a journey together, and as they travelled they used their digging-sticks to gather mai, or vegetable food—fruit, seeds, roots—and grubs. Jindabirrbirr always found plenty of mai, but Kolguru could only find a little. Now it is the hunting law that food gatherers should share everything they find with one another; but Jindabirrbirr would not give any of the mai she found to Kolguru, even though her companion shared the little she gathered each day. As they travelled, Jindabirrbirr grew fat and strong, while Kolguru became thin and weak.

Tchooroo the Great Snake, whose task it was in those far-off days to uphold the law of the tribes, observed Jindabirrbirr's greed, and he knew he must punish her.

One day, as the two women set out for the day's hunting, Jindabirrbirr forgot her digging-stick. She did not miss it until, as they were walking along, Kolguru glanced at her and said, "Where is your digging-stick?"

Then Jindabirrbirr went back alone to the place where they had camped, and fetched it.

While she was away, Tchooroo came gliding through the bush to the place where Kolguru waited for Jindabirrbirr. He lay right across the track that Jindabirrbirr must cross in order to re-join her companion.

Presently Jindabirrbirr came in sight, carrying her digging-stick. When she saw Tchooroo the Great Snake lying there, she stopped, for she was afraid of him.

"Come this way!" Kolguru called from the far side of the track; and she pointed to Tchooroo's head. But Tchooroo moved forward and would not let Jindabirrbirr pass.

"Come that way!" Kolguru called then, pointing to Tchooroo's tail.

But Tchooroo moved back, and then Jindabirrbirr could not pass that way either.

"Jump over him!" Kolguru called; but as soon as Jindabirrbirr ran forward, Tchooroo rose up so that she could not jump high enough.

"Crawl beneath him!" Kolguru called again; but when Jindabirrbirr tried to do that, Tchooroo lay flat, flat along the ground.

So there was no way, no way, no way that Jindabirrbirr could pass.

Then Tchooroo the Great Snake spoke to Jindabirrbirr. "You never shared any of the food you gathered, Jindabirrbirr. And now you must stay for ever where you stand."

And he turned Jindabirrbirr into a big stone which has stood in that place ever since Yamminga times.

Winnini and Kalbain
Emu and Pigeon

In Yamminga times, Winnini the Emu and Kalbain the Pigeon were men. Winnini was a man of the bush, and Kalbain was a seacoast man, and they were enemies. One day they had a great fight. They fought with spears; Kalbain put a stingray string on his spear, and Winnini's spear had a sharp stone point. Winnini also used a long yoong-gara, a throwing-stick. Kalbain did not have a throwing-stick, but he did have a very powerful koorili lanji, a boomerang made from the wood of the koorili tree.

 They fought and fought. Kalbain threw his koorili lanji at Winnini, and it cut both his arms in half. And that is why the emu has such small wings, and can never fly. "You will always have to run along the ground, while I shall be able to fly far, far away!" Kalbain taunted him.

 After Yamminga times, all the dark-haired people of the inland tribes were the enemies of the fair-headed people of the coastal tribes, and they always fought each other, just as Winnini the Emu and Kalbain the Pigeon fought each other long ago.

Ngannamurra Sings
The Mallee Hen Sings

Karraja, a long time ago, a certain man went out hunting each day by himself. He killed plenty of game, which he used to bring back to his camp. Then he would light a fire, cook his meat, make a breakwind for himself, and sleep.

One morning, just at sunrise, the hunter was awakened by the far-off sound of a woman singing very softly. These were the words of her song:

> *The water glistens on the stones in the shade,*
> *Glistens on the stones in the shade —*
> *See how the water glistens!*

The hunter rose up and looked all around his camp, shading his eyes with an outstretched hand, but he could not see the singer. He returned to his fire and cooked some more meat before he went out on his day's hunting.

At sunrise the next day he awoke to hear the same song:

> *The water glistens on the stones in the shade,*
> *Glistens on the stones in the shade —*
> *See how the water glistens!*

But once again, although he looked all around, he could not see the singer. He stole out of his camp and went to the top of a little hill close by; now the singing was louder, and he saw a pile of earth heaped up beside a hole in the hillside. The hunter went close to the hole and called out, "Woman in there! I hear you singing. What are you doing?"

No answer came, but the singing continued, and the hunter could hear someone busy working inside the hill. He crept closer and closer to the hole, until at last his shadow fell across it. Then the singing stopped suddenly and Ngannamurra the Mallee Hen, the woman who was so busy building herself a shelter in the hillside, came rushing out, screaming, "Ngo, ngo, ngo!"

The hunter turned round and fled. He ran a long, long way, and when he had gone, Ngannamurra went back to her song and her building.

And today, Ngannamurra the Mallee Hen still sings her quiet song as she builds her nest.

Langoor and Jalbu
Possum and Native Cat

In Yamminga times, Langoor the Possum and Jalbu the Native Cat both lived in the bush, where they spent their days hunting for food. They kept separate camps. Jalbu was jealous of Langoor, because Langoor was able to use his soft fur to make ornaments. He would take a quantity of his fur and put it on a slab of paperbark, then mix it up with ashes. Then he beat and beat the fur and the ashes with a fire-stick: this made the fur softer still, and very clean and white. When this was done, Langoor the Possum would finger-spin the soft white fur into headbands, armbands and belts, which he wore at the tribal ceremonies, when all the tribesmen danced and sang.

Jalbu wished and wished he could make such fine ornaments out of his hair; but when he tried, he found it was too stiff and straight. All he could do was to make thin lengths of string. He grew very sulky, and one day, when he met Langoor, he began to fight him with his fire-stick. Langoor fought back, also using a fire-stick; the two of them circled round and round each other, looking for chances to strike swift, hard blows.

Langoor's fire-stick was of boonderung wood; it was a stout, crackling stick, and presently he gave Jalbu such a hard blow with it that it made Jalbu's hair twice as stiff and straight as it was before. And now Jalbu could not even make thin lengths of string out of it.

If Jalbu, too, had hit Langoor with a boonderung stick, then Langoor's fur would have become just as stiff and straight as his own. But by mistake Jalbu picked up a fire-stick of jaggal wood, and hit Langoor with that; and it made Langoor's fur even softer and whiter than it was before.

After this, Langoor showed all the womba (tribesmen) how to make ceremonial headbands, armbands and belts out of his fur, and they always used possum fur and never any other.

Lengo and Mandabulabula
The Seacoast Man and his Son

In Yamminga times, Lengo was a Koojangooroo, a seacoast man, and he had one son, who was called Mandabulabula, which means clever and strong.

Lengo was known as the best fisherman of all his people, and in his own country he taught Mandabulabula his son and all the other young men the best way to catch fish. He would break up oysters and other kinds of shellfish into small pieces and throw them into the sea as bait, and then the big fish would come to eat them, and Lengo could kill as many as he wanted. Sometimes he would catch a karrajoo, a small fish like a mullet, cook it over a fire, chew it in his mouth, and then spit it out over the sea. When he did this, the big fish came fast, fast to eat the karrajoonoo — and then Lengo would catch them. It was Lengo, too, who showed the seacoast men how to catch fish by torchlight. He made big woondungoo (torches) that would stay lit a long time, and in the dark he went down to the beach with his lanji (boomerang) to kill all kinds of fish that came in with the tide: walga-walga, salmon; jirra-lool, kingfish, and plenty of others that were good to eat.

Of all the young men whom Lengo taught the skills of fishing, his own son Mandabulabula proved the quickest to learn, until, by the time he reached full manhood, he had become as fine a fisherman as Lengo himself. By this time Lengo had grown old, and so he did not go out to fish any longer, but sent Mandabulabula instead. Each day Mandabulabula would leave camp, and return with plenty of good eating fish strung on his hunting spears — and he would lay down all his catch before his father. Lengo would keep for himself all the best fish that Mandabulabula brought home, and send the next-best fish to his tribal brothers and friends. He left Mandabulabula only the little, stringy fish.

Now it was the law of the seacoast people that full-grown men such as Mandabulabula, who had learnt all the lessons of manhood, had the right to eat any of the fish they caught. Mandabulabula knew this, but because he loved his father, he was obedient to Lengo for a long time, and did not complain when he received only the little, stringy fish out of all those he had caught and brought home.

At last, however, Mandabulabula grew tired of being treated as though he were a woman or a child; he made up his mind that he would no longer catch all those fish for his father to eat and to give away to his tribal brothers and friends. One day, he flung down his portion of no-good fish and strode out of the camp.

"Where are you going?" his father called after him.

Mandabulabula did not reply, so Lengo picked up a spear and followed him as he went down to the beach. There, to his astonishment, Lengo saw his son turn himself into a flash of lightning and vanish over the sea. He tried to stop him with his spear and with boughs from the ground, but Mandabulabula had gone far away from him.

Presently, Mandabulabula turned into red stone and went into the ground near the beach, at a place near Wallaning, north of Broome, which from that time was known to the seacoast men as Mandabulabula-goor, the place where Mandabulabula went into the ground. So Lengo learnt to his sorrow that old men should not forbid their sons, when they are grown to manhood, to take their proper share of the fish they catch.

Walja and Weeloo
Eaglehawk and Curlew

In Dhoogoorr times, Walja the Eaglehawk brought gabbi (water) to Yuria from yamba, yamba weelurarra (the far, far west). He carried it in a kangaroo skin, and put it down at the foot of a big white rock. Then he sat down with his wife, Weeloo the Curlew, beside this waterhole which he had made.

Walja looked all about him, and saw plenty of creatures that would provide meat food: kangaroos, emu, wombat and mallee hen. He saw plenty of trees to provide shade and make fire: mallee, myall and sandalwood, and many plants for vegetable food. Every day he went out hunting for meat, while Weeloo gathered roots and seeds, fruit, ants, lizards, and other small creatures.

Walja and Weeloo lived happily together at Yuria Gabbi for a long time. But one day, when Walja had gone a long way to hunt emu, Koongara the Wattlebird stole up to the camp, where Weeloo was tending the cooking fire. And Koongara took Weeloo away with him to be his wife. The only creatures who saw Koongara take Weeloo were Walja's uncles, the Kaanga (crows), but they did not try to stop him.

Presently, Walja returned from his hunting, carrying a big emu. He saw the empty camp, and felt the cold ashes of the fire. He could not see Weeloo anywhere. He looked all round the camp, and he found the tracks that Koongara had made when he stole up to take Weeloo. Walja knew they were Koongara's tracks, and he saw that they led south.

"I will follow them, and I will kill Koongara and beat Weeloo for letting him take her away," Walja cried out in his anger. Then he sat down on the big white rock that stood beside Yuria Gabbi, and lit a fire to straighten his spear and make it strong and hard and sharp. As he worked, the Kaanga came to mock him.

"Kaa! Kaa!" they sang in their raucous voices. "Koongara and

Weeloo have gone to a far-away camp. Listen! Hear them travel along the road."

Walja did not answer their mocking. He made his spear sharp, sharp, and when it was ready he got up from the rock. And he left behind him on the rock-face the mark of the fire he had kindled, and the imprint of the spear, where he had pressed it down on the stone, and the mark of his knees, where he had sat. Those marks remain on the white rock at Yuria Gabbi to this day. Then he set out in pursuit of Koongara and Weeloo.

Now Walja was a water-bringer: he had brought the water to Yuria, and he was able to make water come from the sky. And presently, as he followed in Koongara's tracks, he gathered together all the big rain-clouds from the west. They came swift, swift, to make rain for him. And he flew up into the rain-clouds as they sped towards Koorijilla, the place where Koongara had fled with Weeloo.

By now Koongara had reached Koorijilla, his own place. Now Koongara already had one wife: Yanguna the White Cockatoo. But Koongara and Yanguna could never agree, for Yanguna always wanted to build her shelter in high, leafy places, while Koongara preferred to live in hollowed-out ground in stony places. Weeloo also liked to make her shelter in stony places, and so Koongara liked her better than Yanguna.

As soon as Koongara reached Koorijilla, he made a deep hollow in the ground and crept into it. He made Weeloo creep in after him, so that if Walja followed them and came to their shelter while they slept, Weeloo would be on top and would be speared first. This might give him time to escape.

By and by, Koongara saw the rain-clouds that Walja had gathered in the sky drawing near. "Here is a great rain coming!" he said. Soon the dark rain-clouds covered all the sky, and so much, so much water fell from them that Koongara could not find a dry place to sit down at Koorijilla. He rose up and took Weeloo on to another place called Waldhabbi, but the rain-clouds followed them there. From Waldhabbi they travelled to Kureengabbi; but still the rain followed them, making a creek of running water all the way behind them.

By now Koongara and Weeloo were very tired; it seemed that there was no place, no place, no place where they might rest. At last they came to a big rock at Kureengabbi, and sat down on it. And here

Walja the Eaglehawk came out from the rain-clouds he had brought all the way from the west; he swooped down upon Koongara the Wattle-bird and speared him. And to this day the big rock at Kureengabbi shows where Koongara's blood flowed over it when he was killed; and the stone is marked with his footprints.

Then Walja took Weeloo the Curlew back to Yuria, his own place, and when the Kaanga, the mocking crows, saw that Walja had found his woman and brought her home, they were silent. At Yuria, Walja beat Weeloo with his club, so hard, so hard, that she cried out, "Weeloo! Weeloo!" over and over again—and that is why the curlew always makes this cry.

Yool-burroo boora . . . all these things happened a long time ago.

The Jandu Who Hunted Wallee
The Women Who Hunted Meat

In Yamminga times, there was once a tribe of jandu (women) who used to live by themselves, at a place called Yardagurra, in the Great Australian Bight. Now it is the law of the tribe that men and women should live together, not separately, and that the men should hunt for wallee (meat) each day, while the women go out to gather mai (vegetable food). But these jandu did not observe the law: not only did they live by themselves, but they went out meat-hunting each day, armed with men's weapons: spears, spear-throwers, and hunting knives. Like men they stalked and speared the kangaroo, and hunted the emu across the plain.

Tchooroo the Great Snake, whose task it was to uphold the law, reproached these women for their way of life. "You should not hunt for wallee," he told them. "That is men's work. You should collect mai. That is women's work and this is the hunting law."

But the women did not take any notice of Tchooroo's words; they went on hunting for meat just as they had done before. When Tchooroo saw that they had not listened to his words, he became angry and turned all the jandu into jiddi joonoo (termites' nests). All the tall, peaked jiddi joonoo which stand now at Yardagurra were once the meat-hunting jandu of Yamminga times, who were punished by Tchooroo the Great Snake because they broke the law of the tribe.

Joord-Joord the Lazy Jandu
Shag the Lazy Woman

In the long-ago Yamminga times, Joord-Joord was a jandu (woman) and she had two sons. Every day her sons went into the bush to hunt langoor (possum) and other meat, and when they brought home their game, they always gave their mother as much as she could eat.

Joord-Joord should also have gone out each day to collect roots and berries and other vegetable food, and to look for bardi and small game such as lizards, for that was a woman's work. But she was fat and lazy, and every day, every day, she gave her two sons nothing but nyell-guru and ngar-ran (white ants and ants' eggs), which she could collect just outside their camp. She would go a short distance and fill her bin-jin (bark vessel) with these, because they were so easy to get. When her sons came home with the langoor or wallaby or goanna they had hunted, every day they saw only the same food in their mother's bin-jin: nyell-guru and ngar-ran. That was all their mother could be bothered to find for them. At last, they grew tired of eating ants and ants' eggs, and one day they threw all the contents of their mother's bin-jin on the fire. As they burned, the ants and the ants' eggs made a loud crackling noise.

"What do I hear burning? What is it?" Joord-Joord called out.

"Nothing," her sons told her. "It is nothing."

And now, every time they came home and found nothing but ants and ants' eggs in Joord-Joord's bin-jin, they burned them.

One day they came home early, bringing fat langoor with them. They found their mother sifting and sifting the nyell-guru and the ngar-ran.

The eldest son said to his brother, "Let us punish our mother, because she does not follow the law of the tribe and bring us proper food. She gives us nothing but that no-good nyell-guru and ngar-ran, while we bring home good meat and always give her a fair share of it."

When Joord-Joord looked up and saw her sons coming towards her, she guessed what was in their minds. "They are going to punish me because I do not go out to collect proper food for them," she thought. She seized her digging-stick and began to hit her sons with it as soon as they drew near. Then each of her sons picked up fire-sticks from the fire and hit their mother on the back. And that is why, when Joord-Joord the Shag became a bird, she had a black back. "Joord-joord! Joord-joord!" she cries as she goes along.

Women should bring home proper vegetable food when their sons fetch good meat for them: that is the law of the tribe.

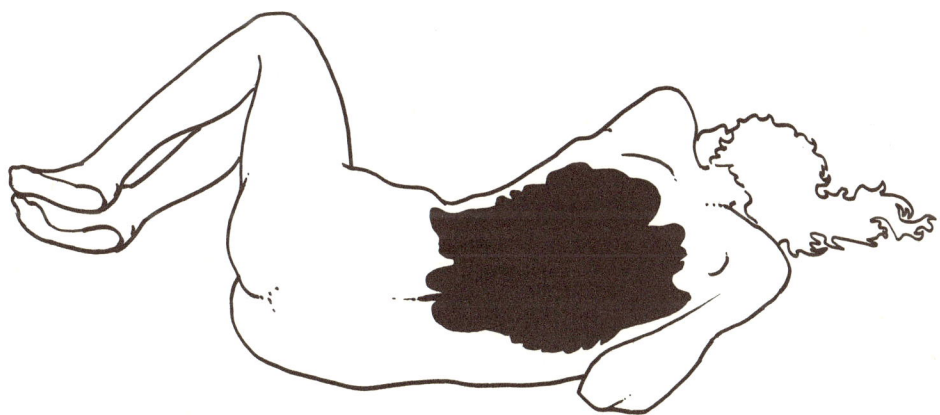

Ngannamurra, Milbarli and Yoongga

Mallee Hen, Short-tailed Goanna and Long-tailed Goanna

In the Dhoogoorr, or Dreamtime, Ngannamurra the Mallee Hen, who was a man in those far-off days, was travelling north when he came to a plain between a group of sandhills covered with mallee and spinifex.

"This shall be my place," he thought. "The sand is firm and good for walking."

He built a shelter there, and then he looked around and saw there was no water. "I will make a waterhole here," he said to himself.

He took out his boomerang and threw it low across the plain. It flew round and round, scooping out the sand as it went, and it made a long, wide waterhole the shape of a carpet-snake's egg.

"This is my waterhole and I will sit down here," Ngannamurra said. So he built his camp and lit his fire and was gwabba gwabba—glad, glad.

Presently Milbarli the short-tailed Goanna and Yoongga the long-tailed Goanna came travelling north in Ngannamurra's tracks. All three were old companions, and when Milbarli and Yoongga arrived at the place where Ngannamurra had built his camp, they said, "We will make more waterholes, so that there will always be plenty and plenty of water here."

Then Milbarli threw his boomerang and made a second waterhole; and Yoongga threw his and made a third waterhole. And Ngannamurra said, "You are my companions and we will never fight or hunt each other, but always build our camps near each other."

And now, wherever Ngannamurra the Mallee Hen makes a nest in the soft sand, close beside it will be the tunnelled nests of Milbarli the short-tailed Goanna and Yoongga the long-tailed Goanna.

Kweenda, Kwidderuk and Wata
Bandicoot, Sparrowhawk and Pigeon

In the Nyitting times of long ago, the yoongar, the men and women who lived in the land, had no fire. In that cold time they shivered and shivered, and every day, every day, they ate their meat raw, because they had no fire to cook it. When the cold waters came down from the sky in the wet season, they would shelter in their huts made of boughs and they would long for the sun to shine down to dry the land and warm them.

Now there was one who did have fire, and that was Kweenda the Bandicoot; but he was a cunning, greedy fellow, and he kept his fire all to himself. He would not let the yoongar have any of it. Every day, when he went out hunting, he carried the fire under his tail.

"Give us some of your fire; share your fire with us!" the yoongar would implore him. But Kweenda would only reply, "What fire? I have no fire."

This answer greatly angered the yoongar, for they could see the fire shining under his tail.

Kwidderuk the Sparrowhawk and his cousin, Wata the Pigeon, sat down to talk one day.

"We must get fire from Kweenda," said Kwidderuk, "so that the yoongar may be warm." And he shivered as he spoke.

"We must get fire from Kweenda," Wata agreed, "so that the yoongar may cook their meat."

Then they both said, "We will go to Kweenda and ask him to give us just a little bit of his fire."

So they went to Kweenda's maia. Kweenda saw them coming, and as they approached he hid the fire in his tail, and began to clean his beard. He had been cooking some meat; it smelt good. Kwidderuk and Wata thought of the raw meat they had eaten that day, and their anger was stirred. They came and sat down beside Kweenda.

"Give us a little bit of your fire, Kweenda," they said.

Kweenda went on cleaning his beard. "I have no fire," he said.

But all the time Kwidderuk and Wata could see the fire shining, shining under his tail.

Then the two of them went away a short distance, and Kwidderuk said, "We will not ask him again; we will take the fire from him to punish him for his cunning and greed."

After this, the two cousins watched Kweenda carefully, and one day they saw him sitting outside his maia with the fire on his back; the smoke was rising from it. Kweenda was smiling; he was happy because he had the fire all to himself. While he was sitting there laughing at his own good fortune, Kwidderuk and Wata came up suddenly and sat down beside him, one on each side. They did not speak to Kweenda the Bandicoot, but they pressed him and pushed him this side and that side, north and south and west; and in this way they travelled and travelled over the ground until at last they came to the sea.

Now Waddarn the Sea was Kweenda's uncle, and when Kwidderuk and Wata had pushed Kweenda to the very brink of the water, he called in a loud voice, "Uncle, uncle, take my fire! Take my fire!" Then, as Kwidderuk and Wata pushed him once more, right into the sea, Kweenda threw his fire to Waddarn his uncle; but a little spark fell out of it onto Wata's beard, and it began to burn.

Kwidderuk and Wata were overjoyed when this happened. They hurried back the way they had come, and from Wata's smouldering beard they put fire into every tree they passed, so that the womba should always be able to find it. They put a lot of fire into the she-oak, the banksia, the jamwood, and blackboy, but only a little into the jarrah and the mahogany.

When the yoongar saw the fire burning in all the trees and the smoke going high, high into the sky, they were gwabba gwabba—glad, glad. They ran towards the trees, dancing and singing.

"Wata and Kwidderuk have got the fire! See the fire! See the fire!" they sang.

Now they could cook their meat and need never again shiver in the cold seasons. They soon discovered that the trees with a lot of fire in them burned well and left good ashes, while those with only a little fire burned slowly and left only charcoal. And now, whenever they travelled, they carried lighted sticks of banksia or jamwood or blackboy with them, for these fire-sticks never died out until the last little bit had burned to ashes. They found, too, that the ashes could be rubbed into spear wounds and make their bodies clean and well.

The yoongar made a corroboree, a song and dance, for Kwidderuk and Wata, which they used to perform so that they and the sons of their sons might always remember who had first brought fire to them.

Ngalloogoo and Koobijet
White Cockatoo and Robin

In Nyitting time, the cold, cold time of long ago, in a place near the sea, a pack of man-eating Janga Dwerda, spirit dingoes, lived in a big cave. Every morning they went out from the cave to go man-hunting; every evening they returned to the cave with their game, which would be either a seacoast man or a river man from the country round about. If they had hunted an old man, then the old dingoes would carry him in their jaws; if their victim were a young man, then the young dingo hunters carried him.

The seacoast and river people were terrified of the savage dogs. They did not dare to light fires to warm themselves or to cook their food, for as soon as the dingoes smelt the fire, they would rush towards it and seize anyone they could find. The people wailed and wept, because they were not strong enough to fight the Janga Dwerda, and because they shivered and shivered in the cold, and had to eat their meat raw.

One day Ngalloogoo the White Cockatoo and his companion Koobijet the Robin sat down together to talk about the Janga Dwerda, and the terrible sorrow that had fallen upon the people, who were all their borungur, their kin.

"Our brothers and uncles, the seacoast men and the river men, shiver with cold and grow thin and weak because of the Janga Dwerda," Ngalloogoo said. "Raw meat is no good for them. We must go and kill those dwerda, so that the people can make fires to warm themselves and cook their food properly."

"Good," said Koobijet. "We will go to the big cave of the Janga Dwerda early tomorrow morning, before they come out, and we will catch them gen-ga-gen — one by one — as they leave the cave. For it has a very little opening, and only one dwerda at a time can come out of it."

Koobijet sounded bold and brave when he said this, but he was

really terrified of the Janga Dwerda. He did not like to tell Ngalloogoo how frightened he was.

At sunrise the next morning Ngalloogoo and Koobijet went to the big cave of the Janga Dwerda. Ngalloogoo waited close by the opening. Koobijet was shaking with fear; he did not dare stand beside Ngalloogoo, but went up into a tree that grew near by, and sat down in its branches. Ngalloogoo was so busy watching the cave, waiting for the dwerda to come out, that he did not notice Koobijet had gone away from him.

Then the first dwerda appeared, poking its muzzle outside the cave. As soon as Ngalloogoo saw it, he sprang forward and hit it on the nose with his dowuk (club). He killed the dwerda with that one blow, and quickly threw it aside. Then he hit the next dwerda to appear, and the next, and the next. He hit each one on the nose and killed it, and threw it aside. And when the biggest and oldest dingo appeared, Ngalloogoo killed him too. Last of all to come out of the cave was a dwerda yog, a woman dingo. But she was cunning; as she put her nose outside, she saw Ngalloogoo raising his dowuk to strike her, and she turned and ran back into the cave. Ngalloogoo ran after her, right into the cave, but although he searched and searched, he could not find her. And that is why dingoes still roam the land today; for if Ngalloogoo had killed that dwerda yog, there would have been no more dingoes.

All this time Koobijet sat trembling among the branches of the tree and watched Ngalloogoo kill all the dwerda, gen-ga-gen. He trembled so much that the tree itself shook, just as if a strong wind were blowing. And even when he saw all the dead dwerda being thrown aside, he was still too frightened to come down to help Ngalloogoo.

Ngalloogoo was very pleased with himself when he had finished killing all the Janga Dwerda; proudly he strode off to the camps of his brothers and uncles, the seacoast men and the river men, singing "jitti-jitti-jitti" all the way. As he reached each camp, he said to the people, "Make your fires and cook your meat, my brothers, for I have killed all the Janga Dwerda except for one little dwerda yog."

Everyone who heard Ngalloogoo's words was goort gwab, glad in his heart, and all the people made a corroboree for Ngalloogoo and Koobijet, dancing and singing their praises. They told their children that they must never hurt or kill their little brothers, Ngalloogoo the White Cockatoo and Koobijet the Robin, who had saved them from the Janga Dwerda. And after that time, the corroboree of Ngalloogoo and Koobijet was always danced at sunrise, the time when Ngalloogoo and Koobijet had gone to the cave of the Janga Dwerda; and the dance showed the people how Ngalloogoo had killed the man-eating dwerda with his dowuk, gen-ga-gen.

Badhu-Wudha and Kurulba
Right-handed One and Left-handed One

In Dhoogoorr times, the men of Willilambi, in the Great Australian Bight, lived in great fear. Walja the Eaglehawk, who lived to the north, was their enemy: he and his woman and their two sons. Whenever Walja came near the camps of the Willilambi, he would give a great shout, and each time he shouted, a boy of the tribe would die. At other times Walja would break a branch from the sandalwood tree, and then, too, one of the boys would die. Soon the Willilambi men were not able to hold any initiation ceremonies, for there were no boys left to take part in them, to learn the secrets of manhood.

Some of the Willilambi men tried to spear Walja, but their spears were too soft, and could not pierce his hard skin. Besides, the tribe was too fearful of Walja to fight him: they were terrified in case the eaglehawk should break the big tree, the Warda, which grew near Willilambi, and which held up the sky. If the Warda were broken, the sky would fall down and darken the earth, and all the men and animals would be killed.

Now in those far-off days there lived two great brothers, Badhu-Wudha, the right-handed one, and Kurulba, the left-handed one. They were spirit beings who used to roam the land. When they saw how Walja the Eaglehawk was killing and killing the Willilámbi boys with his shouting and branch-breaking, they were very sorry.

One day Badhu-Wudha sat down by Willilambi water and said to the tribesmen, "My brother Kurulba and I will kill Walja the Eaglehawk, his woman and their two sons, and when we have done that, we will show you how to make good, hard spears, so that you will be able to fight your enemies in the future."

Badhu-Wudha and Kurulba had very strong spears, hard and smooth, with sharp, sharp points.

The two brothers caused a great wind to spring up from the north, and while it was coming over the plain, they made a big fire, close by the Warda, that great tree that held up the sky. When the fire was burning well, they hid in the other trees near by.

Darkness came with the north wind, and it also swept Walja the Eaglehawk, his woman and their two sons to that place beneath the trees, where they sat down together, folding back their great wings.

"Wommu ngannain—my home," Walja said.

Then he and the woman and their two sons found food, cooked it in the fire, and ate it, and afterwards they hid themselves among the foliage of the trees.

Badhu-Wudha and Kurulba, meanwhile, watched everything they did, and presently the two brothers came creeping, creeping under the Warda. They were so huge that if they had not trodden carefully, the ground would have trembled, the Warda would have broken, and the sky would have fallen to the ground. They came close to the sleeping Walja and his family. Their spears and spear-throwers were ready. Then Badhu-Wudha the right-handed threw his spear at Walja the Eaglehawk, and Kurulba the left-handed threw his spear at Yaggulu Walja, his woman. The two eaglehawks screamed and flew away with the spears piercing their bodies. The young Walja were very frightened, and hid in the trees, but Badhu-Wudha brought them out and killed them on the plain. In a little while Walja and Yaggulu Walja came back to seek their children, and then Badhu-Wudha killed them as well. And the place where the eaglehawks were killed was Cooilgamba; their bones are now the rocks that lie scattered about Wommundo.

After this, Badhu-Wudha and Kurulba caused a great many hardwood trees to spring out of the ground around Willilambi, and they took wood from them and showed the Willilambi men how to make good, strong spears and spear-throwers.

"Now you will always have spears that cannot break, and you need fear the eaglehawk no more," the two brothers told the tribesmen.

The Willilambi men were glad, glad, and after that time they were always able to kill any enemies who preyed upon them. And soon there were plenty of boys in the tribe once more to take part in the initiation ceremonies, and learn the secrets of manhood.

After Badhu-Wudha and Kurulba had delivered the Willilambi from their terror, the two spirit brothers went up into the sky, where

they have been sitting down since Dhoogoorr times, looking like long white clouds: Badhu-Wudha at one side and Kurulba a little distance away. Whenever a Willilambi old man died, Badhu-Wudha would stretch out his right hand and take him up, and whenever a Willilambi woman or child died, Kurulba would reach down for them with his left hand.